Punwani

THE GREAT RAILWAY QUIZ

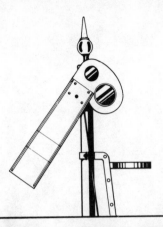

THE GREAT RAILWAY QUIZ

Compiled by
Christopher Hughes
MASTERMIND

David & Charles
Newton Abbot   London   North Pomfret (Vt)

British Library Cataloguing in Publication Data
Hughes, Christopher
The great railway quiz.
1. Railroads—Great Britain—History—
Miscellanea
I. Title
385'.0941   HE3018
ISBN 0-7153-8596-8

Technical consultants
Anthony J. Lambert and
Geoffrey Kichenside

Phototypeset by ABM (Typographics) Ltd, Hull
and printed in Great Britain
by Billings & Sons Ltd, Worcester
for David & Charles (Publishers) Limited
Brunel House   Newton Abbot   Devon

Published in the United States of America
by David & Charles Inc
North Pomfret   Vermont 05053   USA

Contents

To Rachel

Introduction

Since winning the BBCtv Mastermind competition in 1983, I have frequently been asked how I, a former grammar school drop-out, ex-British Railways fireman and London Transport train driver, have managed to amass sufficient knowledge over the years to be able to beat some of the finest brains in the land at what is, after all, the most heavily intellectual of all British quiz shows. I wish I knew the answer to that one . . .

As many readers will remember, the main specialist subject which I took on Mastermind was 'British Steam Locomotives from 1900 to 1968' which at once captured the attention of the vast army of railway enthusiasts, most of whom, I'm sure, could have answered the questions at least as well as I did. However, the skill—and I believe it can fairly be described as a skill—with Mastermind is to be able to clear your mind of all distractions, listen carefully to Magnus Magnusson's questions, and not allow yourself to be intimidated by the paraphernalia of television.

I first became interested in railways in about 1949 or '50 when I was a toddler living in Welwyn Garden City, within sound—if not sight—of the East Coast main line. I passed through all the usual phases of trainspotting with the inevitable dog-eared Ian Allan ABCs until, at the age of about ten, having by then moved to Waltham Cross on the erstwhile Great Eastern Railway, I discovered in the public library at Cheshunt a copy of Hamilton-Ellis's *Some Classic Locomotives* which opened my eyes to the fact that there was a lot more to the study of locomotives than dashing home from school every day to see which locomotive was hauling the *Fenman* through Waltham Cross that afternoon. At school I was a totally mediocre performer, eventually deciding at the age of fifteen that the academic life held no attractions for me whatsoever and, after various vicissitudes, joined British Railways as an engine cleaner at the old Motive Power Depot at Hornsey, where I was soon promoted to the grade of fireman, just in time to catch the last few months of steam working on the southern end of the East Coast main line. In fact this was represented by a rather sad procession of decrepit 9Fs, B1s and such like, but to a sixteen-year-old fireman it was the stuff of life itself. It was during this period that my railway education was completed, mostly by the kindness of the drivers with whom I worked, particularly the late Stan Jeffries to whom I shall always be grateful for his crystal clear explanations of the finer technical points of the steam locomotive.

Increasing dissatisfaction with the way that British Rail was going in the late 'sixties, and feeling no particular loyalty to a railway changed out of all recognition in a few short years, led me to transfer in 1970 to London Transport, where I worked my way up from guard to driver on the Piccadilly Line.

Never having had any pretensions towards authorship, I was surprised and gratified to be approached by David & Charles with a view to compiling a quiz book on railways, which I have finally—after several false starts and several gallons of midnight oil—completed. The questions have been designed to stretch the memory and the reference library as much as possible, so have a go at some of these and remember, as Magnus Magnusson says before every round of Mastermind, 'It's only a game'. . .

CHRISTOPHER HUGHES

Ponders End
Middlesex
January 1984

British Steam Locomotives

answers on pp 96-103

1 What was the working pressure of *Rocket*'s original boiler?

2 How many copper firetubes, 3in in diameter, were fitted to *Rocket*'s original boiler?

3 Who was the famous builder of road coaches who was commissioned by Robert Stephenson & Co to build the tender for *Rocket?*

4 What was used as a water tank on the tender built for *Rocket* in 1829?

5 What was the maximum speed achieved by Timothy Hackworth's *Sans Pareil* in the course of the Rainhill Trials?

6 What were the names of the two engineers who entered *Novelty* for the Rainhill Trials?

7 How was T. S. Brandreth's Rainhill entry, *Cycloped*, propelled?

8 What was the name of the engine entered by Timothy Burstall for the Rainhill Trials and which proved an abject failure?

9 Which of the Liverpool & Manchester Railway engines was used to convey the injured William Huskisson, MP, to hospital at St Helens from the scene of his accident during the opening ceremony?

10 What name was given to the first locomotive built for the Canterbury & Whitstable Railway by Robert Stephenson & Co?

11 In which locomotive built by Robert Stephenson & Co for the Liverpool & Manchester Railway in 1830 did the combination of cylinders beneath the smokebox and outside sandwich frames first appear?

12 What was the wheel arrangement of the Stephenson

Patentee type of locomotive, widely sold at home and abroad?

13   To which railway did the Liverpool & Manchester Railway sell the heavily rebuilt *Rocket* in 1836?

14   Which firm built the famous 0-4-2 goods engine *Lion* for the Liverpool & Manchester Railway in 1838?

15   The Stephenson 2-2-2 *North Star* came to the Great Western Railway as a frustrated export order. For which foreign railway had the engine been originally intended?

16   What was the name of the first locomotive to be tried in steam on the Great Western Railway, on 28 December 1837?

17   The Stephenson 2-2-2 *North Star* worked the first train on the Great Western Railway, for the directors, on 31 May 1838. Which engine worked the first public train, four days later?

18   Who designed the freakish locomotives *Hurricane* and *Thunderer*, with engines and boilers on separate chassis, which proved failures on the Great Western Railway in 1838–9?

19   How did *Morning Star* differ from *North Star* and the other ten Star class locomotives delivered to the Great Western Railway in 1839–41?

20   Which was the first locomotive to be built at Crewe by the London & North Western Railway, in early 1845?

21   Which was the first locomotive to be built entirely at the Great Western Railway's works at Swindon, in 1846?

22   Who designed the 2-2-2 *Cornwall*, with 8ft 6in driving wheels, built at Crewe in 1847?

23   The Southern Division of the London & North Western Railway had two large Crampton-type locomotives, *London*, built by Tulk & Ley in 1847, and *Liverpool*. Which firm built *Liverpool* in 1848?

24   The first engines delivered to the Bristol & Exeter Railway in 1849 were essentially a small version of Gooch's

Iron Duke class on the Great Western Railway. Which Bristol firm built the first ten Bristol & Exeter engines?

25 Which Great Western Railway Iron Duke class 4-2-2 by Gooch was exhibited at the Crystal Palace in Hyde Park in 1851?

26 What number was carried by the large 4-2-2 engine built by R. & W. Hawthorn for the Great Northern Railway, to the design of Archibald Sturrock, with a view to the inauguration of a service from King's Cross to Edinburgh in eight hours?

27 In 1859 the London & North Western Railway, as successors to the Liverpool & Manchester Railway, sold the 0-4-2 *Lion*. To whom and for what purpose?

28 How many of John Ramsbottom's DX class 0-6-0 goods engines were built at Crewe between 1858–72?

29 For which English railway did Robert Stephenson & Co build two 4-4-0 locomotives, *Brougham* and *Lowther*, with large, side-window cabs and other modern features in 1860?

30 For which British railway were W. Fairbairn & Sons still building the archaic Bury type of 0-4-0 tender engines as late as 1861?

31 How many of Stirling's famous 8ft Singles were built for the Great Northern Railway between 1870–95?

32 Which were the first 4-4-0 locomotives to be built in the United Kingdom with inside plate frames and inside cylinders, the genesis of a breed of locomotives recognised as characteristically British?

33 Which was the first of William Stroudley's famous London, Brighton & South Coast Railway A1 class 0-6-0 tank engines to enter service in October 1872?

34 In 1873 David Jones rebuilt two old Highland Railway engines, Nos 7 and 10, as 4-4-0s. Which famous class was developed from these rebuilt engines?

35 Which was the first locomotive with Walschaert's valve gear to run in Great Britain?

36   Until 1876 the first twenty-four Beyer Peacock 4-4-0Ts on the Metropolitan District Railway were not numbered. How were they identified?

37   For which British railway did Beyer Peacock & Co of Manchester build a class of massive 0-6-4Ts with 4ft 7in driving wheels, 21½in x 26in cylinders and 150psi boiler pressure in 1885?

38   Where was the unique 4-2-2 engine built by Neilson & Co of Glasgow, and subsequently taken over by the Caledonian Railway as their No 123, originally exhibited?

39   By what nickname were Webb's 18in goods engines with 5ft 2½in driving wheels and Joy valve gear, introduced on the London & North Western Railway in 1887, generally known?

40   In the Webb three-cylinder compounds of the London & North Western Railway, the valves of the outside high-pressure cylinders were operated by a form of Joy valve gear. How was the valve of the inside, low-pressure cylinder operated?

41   What was the system of compounding in the North Eastern Railway J class 4-2-2s of 1888 before rebuilding as simple engines in 1894–5?

42   In 1889 the Barry Railway bought two 0-8-0s from Sharp Stewart & Co. For which foreign railway had they originally been built?

43   Which of James Stirling's 4-4-0 express locomotives did the South Eastern Railway exhibit at the 1889 Paris International Exhibition?

44   How many of Barton Wright's 'Ironclad' 0-6-0s on the Lancashire & Yorkshire Railway were rebuilt as saddle tank shunting engines between 1891–1900 by John Aspinall?

45   Which was the first locomotive to be built for a British railway with a Belpaire firebox, a Belgian design allowing more steam space and simplifying the staying of the plates?

46   Which was the last Great Western Railway engine to

be built for the broad gauge?

47   Which Great Western Railway broad gauge engine worked the 5.00pm Paddington to Plymouth train on 20 May 1892, the last broad gauge train to leave Paddington?

48   What were the names of the two Great Western Railway broad gauge tank locomotives retained at Swindon until 1894 to shunt condemned broad gauge rolling stock following final gauge conversion?

49   Which was the first of J. Holden's Great Eastern Railway T19 class 2-4-0s to be converted to an oil burner, in 1893, and what name did she carry in her modified state?

50   For which railway did David Jones build the first 4-6-0 locomotives to run in the United Kingdom, his 'Big Goods' class of 1894?

51   What was the diameter of the coupled wheels of the two North Eastern Railway Q1 class 4-4-0s, Nos 1869 and 1870, built at Gateshead in 1896?

52   For which Scottish railway did James Manson design a four-cylinder 4-4-0, No 11, in 1897?

53   Which was the first London & South Western Railway locomotive to incorporate Dugald Drummond's firebox water tubes, and in what other respect was this engine unusual?

54   Which Webb Teutonic class three-cylinder compound 2-2-2-0 worked the 2.00pm Corridor train from Euston to Crewe almost without a break from 1891–9?

55   Which were the last 4-2-2 locomotives to be delivered to a British railway?

56   What performance criteria was J. Holden's 0-10-0T No 20, known as the 'Decapod' and built for the Great Eastern Railway at Stratford in 1902, designed to fulfil?

57   Which Badminton class 4-4-0 emerged from Swindon works in 1903 fitted with a massive boiler, 5ft 5in in diameter, and a commodious side-window cab?

58   Which Great Western Railway engine is reputed to

have reached a speed of 102.3mph while descending Wellington bank, near Taunton, in 1904?

59 From which long-established firm of locomotive builders did the Great Northern Railway take delivery of a four-cylinder compound 4-4-2, No 1300, on 26 June 1905?

60 To what more useful form was J. Holden's Great Eastern Railway 0-10-0T No 20 (the 'Decapod') rebuilt at Stratford works in 1906?

61 Between 1907–10, G. J. Churchward rebuilt twenty Great Western Railway 2301 class 0-6-0 goods engines in a completely different form. What guise did these engines take?

62 What nickname was given to those engines of Holden's Great Eastern Railway T19 class which were rebuilt with large diameter boilers from 1908, the name arising from their foreshortened appearance?

63 Which were the last of Webb's London & North Western Railway three-cylinder compound locomotives to remain in service?

64 Which was the last class of locomotive to be built for the London & South Western Railway to the design of Dugald Drummond?

65 What type of cylinder arrangement, more usually found on large stationary engines, was fitted to the North Eastern Railway S2 class 4-6-0 No 825 by Sir Vincent Raven in 1913?

66 From which manufacturer did the South Eastern & Chatham Railway take delivery of a batch of L class 4-4-0s in June 1914?

67 What name was carried by Great Western Railway Star class 4-6-0 No 4017 *Knight of Liège* prior to August 1914?

68 By what inexplicable nickname did Glasgow & South Western Railway enginemen know Peter Drummond's '16' class 2-6-0s, introduced in 1915?

69   Which was the last London, Brighton & South Coast Railway engine to retain the Stroudley Improved Engine Green livery, until 1917?

70   After Holden's 'Decapod', built by the Great Eastern Railway in 1902, which was the second ten-coupled engine to be built for a British railway?

71   Which was H. N. Gresley's first Great Northern Railway three-cylinder locomotive incorporating Gresley's own form of conjugated valve gear, rather than the later Gresley/Holcroft arrangement?

72   At the end of World War I, where did the British Government order the construction of 100 of R. E. L. Maunsell's South Eastern & Chatham Railway N class 2-6-0s, chiefly to absorb excess manufacturing capacity?

73   What was the number and name of the London, Brighton & South Coast Railway L class 4-6-4T that served as the company's war memorial?

74   In 1923, why did the London Midland & Scottish Railway number one of the former Lancashire & Yorkshire Railway 2-4-2Ts as No 6762, instead of its sequential number, 10638?

75   Which Great Western Railway Saint class 4-6-0 was rebuilt in 1924 with 6ft diameter driving wheels as the prototype for the Hall class, built from 1928?

76   Which was the first four-cylinder tank engine to run on a British railway?

77   Which were the only two Midland Railway locomotives to bear names?

78   Commencing in 1924, the London & North Eastern Railway built twenty-four engines to a slightly modified design of the former Great Central Railway Director class 4-4-0s. To which part of the system were these engines sent?

79   Which locomotives were nicknamed 'Tishies' by railwaymen after a popular cartoon racehorse of the time, always depicted with his front legs crossed?

80   What name was given to the Castle class 4-6-0 built at Swindon in 1924 which incorporated a large number of parts from the scrapped Churchward 4-6-2 No 111 *The Great Bear?*

81   After the grouping, which of the former Great Northern Railway Ivatt C1 class 4-4-2s was fitted by H. N. Gresley with a booster, supplied by the Franklin Railway Supply Co of New York, in July 1923?

82   Which was the first of Churchward's Great Western Railway Star class 4-6-0s to be rebuilt as a Castle class engine by C. B. Collett in 1925, and what name and number was this engine given in January 1936?

83   For what particular purpose did the London & North Eastern Railway order the unique U1 class 2-8-8-2 Garratt locomotive from Beyer Peacock & Co of Manchester?

84   Which Great Western Railway Castle class 4-6-0 went to the London & North Eastern Railway for trials against A1 class Pacific No 4475 in 1925?

85   Which of R. E. L. Maunsell's Southern Railway four-cylinder Lord Nelson class 4-6-0s had 6ft 3in diameter driving wheels, unlike the other fifteen members of the class which had 6ft 7in diameter driving wheels?

86   Which two London & North Eastern Railway locomotives were fitted with large E-type superheaters, designed by the Superheater Co of New York, in 1925-6?

87   Which was the last former London & North Western Railway Webb four-cylinder compound locomotive to remain in service with the London Midland & Scottish Railway?

88   What was the heaviest type of 4-4-0 locomotive to run in Great Britain, prior to the introduction in 1927 of H. N. Gresley's D49 class on the London & North Eastern Railway?

89   How many corridor tenders were built at Doncaster works for coupling to Gresley A1 Pacifics in anticipation of the inauguration of the non-stop 'Flying Scotsman' service on 1 May 1928?

90   Of the thirty-three Garratt locomotives built for the London Midland & Scottish Railway by Beyer Peacock & Co in 1927–30, how many were fitted with vacuum brakes?

91   What classification was given to Maunsell's heavy 0-8-0Ts built for the Southern Railway in 1929?

92   What was the number and name of the experimental London Midland & Scottish Railway 4-6-0 with the high-pressure, semi-water tube boiler built by the North British Locomotive Co in 1929?

93   What was the working pressure of the Yarrow water tube boiler fitted to the London & North Eastern Railway four-cylinder compound 4-6-4 No 10000 by Gresley in 1929?

94   On completion of the Southern Railway's electrification of the main line to Brighton, the large L class 4-6-4Ts were redundant. To what more useful wheel configuration were they rebuilt?

95   Which Royal Scot class 4-6-0 of the London Midland & Scottish Railway toured the USA in 1933, masquerading as No 6100 *Royal Scot?*

96   Which was the last former London & North Western Railway Precedent class 2-4-0 to remain in service on the London Midland & Scottish Railway?

97   Which two Great Western Railway locomotives were disfigured by a singularly ugly form of semi-streamlining in 1935?

98   Which was the last 4-2-2 tender locomotive to work in ordinary passenger service in the United Kingdom?

99   What was the maximum speed achieved by London & North Eastern Railway A4 class Pacific No 2509 *Silver Link* while hauling a special press demonstration train on 27 September 1935?

100   Which Great Western Railway Duke class 4-4-0 was rebuilt with the frames from scrapped Bulldog class 4-4-0 No 3365 to form the prototype for the Dukedog rebuilds which began in 1936?

101   Which was the last engine with composite wood and steel sandwich frames to run on a British main line railway?

102   Which London & North Eastern Railway A3 class Pacific was the first to be fitted with a Kylchap (Kylala-Chapelon) double blastpipe and chimney in 1937?

103   What number was carried by the first of O. V. S. Bulleid's Q1 class 0-6-0 when it first appeared on the Southern Railway in 1942?

104   What was the last design of locomotive by Sir Nigel Gresley to enter service on the London & North Eastern Railway?

105   Which of Gresley's London & North Eastern Railway three-cylinder D49 class 4-4-0s did Edward Thompson rebuild in 1942 as a two-cylinder locomotive?

106   How many of Edward Thompson's B1 class 4-6-0s were built for the London & North Eastern Railway and British Railways between 1942–50?

107   How many London Midland & Scottish Railway 3F class 0-6-0Ts were regauged to 5ft 3in in 1944 and transferred to Northern Counties Comittee in Northern Ireland, forming NCC class Y.

108   What was the name given to London Midland & Scottish Railway class 5MT 4-6-0 No 5155 in 1942, the name being removed in 1944?

109   What was the War Department number of the Austerity 2-8-0 which was badly damaged in the explosion at Soham, Cambridgeshire, on 2 June 1944?

110   The Southern Railway retained two former London & South Western Railway 0415 class 4-4-2Ts for working the Lyme Regis branch. From what source were they able to purchase a third such engine in 1946?

111   What devices were fitted in the fireboxes of the Southern Railway Bulleid Pacifics to assist water circulation?

112   Why were the small Collett 0-4-2Ts of the Great

Western Railway 4800 class, Nos 4800-74, renumbered as 1400-74 from 1946 onwards?

113   To which other engine of the same class did the London & North Eastern Railway transfer the nameplates from the scrapped D16/3 class 4-4-0 No 2500 *Claud Hamilton* in 1947?

114   In February 1948, which former Great Western King class 4-6-0 was the first to be fitted at Swindon with the larger four-row superheater in place of the original arrangement?

115   Which was the last former London & North Eastern Railway A10 (formerly class A1) Pacific to be rebuilt with a 220psi boiler, making the engine an A3, in December 1948?

116   Between 1935-46, which former London & South Western Railway Drummond T9 class 4-4-0 was kept in immaculate external condition by the Southern Railway for working royal trains, and similar duties?

117   Which was the last of the former London Midland & Scottish Railway Princess Coronation class Pacifics to run with the original streamlined casing?

118   On the London Midland Region of British Railways, which Patriot class 4-6-0 was the last to be converted to class 7P, with a type 2A taper boiler, in 1949?

119   What was unusual about class 5MT 4-6-0s Nos 44718-27, built for the London Midland Region of British Railways at Crewe in 1949?

120   What caused the premature scrapping of former London & South Western Railway M7 class 0-4-4T No 672 in May 1948?

121   Only one of O. V. S. Bulleid's revolutionary Leader class 0-6-6-0s ever worked in steam on the Southern Region of British Railways. How many others were under construction when the project was terminated?

122   Which of the former London, Brighton & South Coast Railway H1 class Atlantics was used by O. V. S. Bulleid as a test bed for experiments with sleeve valves, in-

tended for use in the Leader class, during 1948–50?

123   Which former London Midland & Scottish Railway works built the last two class 5MT 4-6-0s in 1951, bringing the class total to 842, the engines concerned having Caprotti valve gear and Skefco roller bearings throughout?

124   How did former London Midland & Scottish Railway Princess Royal class Pacific No 46205 *Princess Victoria* differ from the other members of the class?

125   Which British Railways works built all fifty-five of Riddles' 7MT Britannia class Pacifics between 1951–4?

126   What name was given to former London Midland & Scottish Railway Jubilee class 4-6-0 No 45700 in 1951, freeing her original name for use on the first of the British Railways Standard 7MT class Pacifics?

127   Where and on what date did the brand new British Railways Standard 7MT class Pacific receive the name *Britannia?*

128   Where was British Railways Standard 7MT class Pacific No 70004 *William Shakespeare* exhibited during 1951?

129   Which of the British Railways Standard 7MT class Pacifics were delivered in 1953 fitted with Westinghouse air brake equipment, in addition to the usual vacuum and steam brake equipment?

130   The unique British Railways class 8P Pacific No 71000 *Duke of Gloucester* was specifically authorised as a direct replacement for which, equally unique, locomotive?

131   Nearly all the British Railways 7MT class Pacifics were named on delivery, or very soon afterwards. One locomotive, however, never received a name. What was the number of this engine?

132   Which was the last Royal Scot class 4-6-0 on the London Midland Region of British Railways to have its parallel boiler replaced by the type 2A taper boiler?

133   Which was the first of Bulleid's Merchant Navy

class Pacifics to lose its streamlined casing, in 1956, and to be given conventional Walschaert's valve gear in place of the chain-driven Bulleid arrangement?

134   Which was the last of the former London, Brighton & South Coast Railway D1 class 0-4-2Ts to remain in existence?

135   How many of the British Railways Standard 9F class 2-10-0s were built with the Italian Crosti boiler and feed water heating arrangement?

136   What apparatus of American origin was fitted to three British Railways 9F class 2-10-0s, Nos 92165-7, in 1958?

137   Which class of former London & North Eastern Railway 0-6-2Ts virtually monopolised the suburban workings to Enfield and Chingford from Liverpool Street, until the services were electrified in November 1960?

138   What modification was made to British Railways Standard 9F class 2-10-0 No 92250, the last steam engine built at Crewe, after approximately one year in service?

139   Which was the last former London & North Eastern Railway Gresley A3 class Pacific to remain in service with British Railways, being withdrawn in January 1966?

140   Between 1951–2, ten British Railways Standard 6MT, or Clan, class Pacifics were built for the Scottish Region. How many more of these engines was it proposed to build, for both Scottish and Southern regions, before the order was rescinded?

141   What was the last class of 0-4-4T to be built in Britain?

142   What was the name given to the Great Central Railway engine that commemorated the company's fallen in World War I?

143   Which class of engine was commonly accepted as bearing the nickname of 'Paddleboxes' on account of their huge splashers?

144   In March 1903 the London & South Western Rail-

way purchased two locomotives from another British railway company for use on the sharply curved Lyme Regis branch. What class of engine were they?

145   By the 1860s the 0-4-0 tender locomotive was a rarity. Which British railway company built a pair of them, with inside cylinders, during that decade and gave them the numbers 357 and 358?

PRIZE QUESTIONS
British Steam Locomotives
(indicate the correct answer on the entry form on page 131)

Q1 Which Great Western Railway locomotive hauled the train in which Queen Victoria first travelled by railway, on 13 June 1842, from Slough to Paddington?

A *Actaeon.*
B *Phlegethon.*
C *Lucifer.*
D *Mazeppa.*

Q2 What was the number of the London & North Western Railway 'Bloomer' 2-2-2 which made a record run from Stafford to Euston with diplomatic despatches at the time of the 'Trent' incident during the American Civil War, in 1862?

A 372.
B 895.
C 204.
D 109.

Q3 The Metropolitan Railway bought five powerful 0-6-0Ts in 1868, for working the St John's Wood extension from Baker Street. Which firm built these engines?

A Beyer Peacock, Manchester.
B Slaughter, Gruning, Bristol.
C Robert Stephenson & Co, Newcastle.
D Worcester Engine Co, Worcester.

Q4 What was the number of the North British locomotive driven on to the Forth Bridge by the Marchioness of Tweeddale at the bridge's opening ceremony?

A 224.
B 602.
C 262.
D 213.

Q5 Which French engineering concern built the three De Glehn compound Atlantics imported by the Great Western Railway in 1903–5?

A S.A.C.M., Mulhouse.

B S.A.C.M., Belfort.
C Schnieder, Le Creusot.
D Corpet-Louvet, Paris.

Q6 What type of feed water heater and pump was fitted to LNER B12 class 4-6-0 No 8509 in February 1926?

A A.C.F.I.
B Dabeg.
C Knorr.
D Worthington Simpson.

Q7 What name was unofficially bestowed upon Southern Railway L class 4-4-0 No 763 by volunteers during the 1926 General Strike and was carried, neatly painted, on the engine's splashers for several months?

A *Betty Baldwin.*
B *Lloyd George.*
C *King George V.*
D *Ramsey MacDonald.*

Q8 Who was responsible for the design of the experimental eight-cylinder 2-6-2 No 2299, which ran a few unsuccessful trials on the Midland Railway in 1908?

A Henry Fowler.
B R. M. Deeley.
C Cecil Paget.
D David Bain.

Q9 Which former London & North Western Railway Claughton class 4-6-0 was nominally rebuilt as the prototype of the Patriot or 'Baby Scot' class in 1930, very little of the original engine remaining in the rebuilt locomotive?

A No 5945 *Ingestre.*
B No 5971 *Croxteth.*
C No 5925 *E. C. Trench.*
D No 5964 *Patriot.*

Q10 British Railways Standard 9F 2-10-0s Nos 92178 and 92183-250 were built with double chimneys. How many other 9Fs were subsequently fitted with double chimneys?

A Twelve.
B Nine.
C Four.
D Six.

Q11 In 1891 the Uruguay Eastern Railway refused delivery of two 4-4-0Ts from Dübs & Co. Which British railway company, on which the engines were nicknamed 'Yankee' tanks, bought them, ordering three more in 1893?

A Barry Railway.
B London, Chatham & Dover Railway.
C Highland Railway.
D Furness Railway.

Q12 In 1909, which London & North Western Railway Precursor class 4-4-0 was involved in trials against the superheated Marsh 13 class 4-4-2Ts, working the *Sunny South Express*, on the London, Brighton & South Coast Railway?

A No 1433 *Faerie Queen*.
B No 7 *Titan*.
C No 1784 *Python*.
D No 659 *Dreadnought*.

Q13 From which railway did the Great Western Railway acquire the small 2-4-0T No 1308 *Lady Margaret* in 1909, the engine having been built by Andrew Barclay & Co of Kilmarnock in 1902?

A The Lambourn Valley Railway.
B The Liskeard & Caradon Railway.
C The Liskeard & Looe Railway.
D The Llanelly Railway & Dock Co.

Q14 From which locomotive builders did the Hull & Barnsley Railway obtain five 4-4-0 locomotives, designated Class J, to the design of Matthew Stirling, in 1910?

A North British Locomotive Co, Glasgow.
B Kitson & Co, Leeds.
C Robert Stephenson & Co, Newcastle.
D Beyer Peacock & Co, Manchester.

Q15 Which was the first London & North Eastern Railway Gresley Pacific to be built at Doncaster as a class A3 with 220psi boiler and 19in diameter cylinders?

A No 2743 *Felstead*.
B No 2500 *Windsor Lad*.
C No 2750 *Papyrus*.
D No 2796 *Spearmint*.

Q16   What form of rotary cam poppet valve gear was fitted by the London Midland & Scottish Railway to five of the Hughes 6P5F 2-6-0s in 1931?

A   Lentz.
B   Caprotti.
C   British Caprotti.
D   Reidinger.

Q17   Which Great Western Railway Saint class 4-6-0 emerged from Swindon works in May 1931 fitted with Caprotti rotary cam poppet valve gear?

A   No 2932 *Ashton Court*.
B   No 2936 *Cefntilla Court*.
C   No 2939 *Croome Court*.
D   No 2935 *Caynham Court*.

Q18   What name was carried by the large 0-8-0T built by Hawthorn Leslie & Co for the Kent & East Sussex Railway and acquired by the Southern Railway in 1932 in exchange for two old Beattie saddle tanks?

A   *Titania*.
B   *Circe*.
C   *Hecate*.
D   *Pandora*.

Q19   In September 1958, the Eastern Region withdrew B2 class 4-6-0 No 61671 *Royal Sovereign*, used for working royal trains. To which other engine of the same class were the nameplates transferred?

A   No 61615 *Culford Hall*.
B   No 61616 *Fallodon*.
C   No 61632 *Belvoir Castle*.
D   No 61672 *West Ham United*.

Q20   On 8 June 1961, which A4 Pacific hauled the royal train from King's Cross to York on the occasion of the wedding of the Duke of Kent?

A   No 60022 *Mallard*.
B   No 60007 *Sir Nigel Gresley*.
C   No 60014 *Silver Link*.
D   No 60028 *Walter K. Whigham*.

British Railway History

answers on pp 104-109

1   Who built what is thought to have been England's first wooden 'railway', from Strelley to Wollaton near Nottingham, in 1603–4?

2   When was the first recorded use of the word 'railway'?

3   Where was the earliest railway in Scotland, known to have been working in 1722?

4   When did the first portion of the famous Tanfield Wagonway in County Durham commence operation?

5   Who was the entrepreneur and Post Office reformer who built a wooden wagonway at Prior Park, Bath, in 1731?

6   Which was the first railway to be authorised by Act of Parliament?

7   What was the date of the opening of the Stockton & Darlington Railway?

8   When was the London & Southampton Railway Co incorporated?

9   How was it possible for the Great Western Railway to be built as a broad gauge line, despite a Parliamentary requirement for all railway bills to include a clause requiring the line to be built to standard gauge?

10   On what date did the Great Western Railway Act receive the Royal Assent?

11   What was the name of the stationmaster at Milton on the Newcastle & Carlisle Railway who invented the card railway ticket in 1836?

12   Between which two points did the first section of the Great Western Railway open to the public on 31 May 1838?

13   What form of traction was used on the London &

Blackwall Railway, opened from Minories to Blackwall in 1840?

14   In 1840 it was possible to travel from Euston to Glasgow in 20½ hours. How was the middle section of the journey covered?

15   On what date did the Great Western Railway open throughout from London to Bristol?

16   On what date was the rail route from Euston to York via Rugby completed with the opening of the last section of the main line of the York & North Midland Railway, between Burton Salmon and Masborough?

17   Where in London was the original terminus of the Eastern Counties Railway?

18   What was the name of the railway opened for mineral traffic on 4 January 1841, and for passengers on 30 March, between York and Darlington?

19   When did the first section of the Bristol & Exeter Railway open between Bristol and Bridgwater?

20   Which town was reached by the main line of the Bristol & Exeter Railway on 1 July 1842?

21   On which small railway did the London & South Western Railway take out a lease, for strategic reasons, in 1845?

22   Which was the first section of the Great Northern Railway to open, on 1 March 1848?

23   How long did the 10.00am train from King's Cross (later named the *Flying Scotsman*) take to reach Edinburgh in 1862?

24   When did the Great Eastern Railway open the new terminus at Liverpool Street in London to local traffic, main line traffic following nearly two years later?

25   Which two railway companies jointly owned the Severn & Wye Railway and the Severn Bridge?

26   When did the first Great Western Railway coal train

pass through the Severn Tunnel?

27   In which year did the Great Eastern Railway's Harwich Continental services become a Royal Mail route?

28   In which year was the first section of the London & South Western Railway electrified on the third-rail system, as later adopted by the Southern Railway?

29   When did the *Brighton Belle*, the only electric multiple-unit Pullman train in the world, make its last run between Victoria and Brighton?

30   In what year did the Grand Junction Railway make the first Travelling Post Office experiments with a converted horse box fitted up for the sorting of mail *en route?*

31   When was the first proposal for a horse-worked railway between London and Bristol, made by Dr James Anderson.

32   What was the furthest point south reached by the Croydon, Merstham & Godstone Railway, an independent extension of the pioneer horse-worked Surrey Iron Railway?

33   When did the Oystermouth Railway near Swansea officially open to passengers?

34   Who was the great Quaker entrepreneur active in the promotion of the Stockton & Darlington Railway?

35   Who was chairman of the Stockton & Darlington Railway at the start of construction?

36   Which town was linked to Stratford-upon-Avon by a horse-worked standard gauge tramway in 1826?

37   On what date were both the London & Birmingham and the Grand Junction railways incorporated?

38   Pending completion of Kilsby Tunnel, between which two points on the London & Birmingham Railway were passengers ferried by road coaches?

39   Where was the first place at which the broad gauge Great Western Railway came into contact with a standard

gauge railway, creating transhipment problems?

40   In what year did the South Eastern Railway acquire a lease on the Canterbury & Whitstable Railway?

41   Which two undertakings amalgamated on 21 July 1845 to form the St Helens Canal & Railway Co?

42   Who was the headmaster of Eton College who attempted to obtain the assistance of W. E. Gladstone to prevent the construction of the Windsor branch of the Great Western Railway, passing close to the college.

43   When did the London & North Western Railway open the Trent Valley line, thereby avoiding Birmingham.

44   Which railway in the London area briefly operated by atmospheric traction at about the same time as the South Devon Railway?

45   When was the inaugural journey of the *Irish Mail* from Euston?

46   Between which two places did the Midland Railway exercise running powers over the Great Northern Railway main line from 1858–68?

47   Which broad gauge railway was leased jointly by the Great Western, Bristol & Exeter and South Devon railways from its opening on 4 May 1859?

48   In which year was the 'Waverley' route between Edinburgh and Carlisle completed, on the opening of the Border Union Railway between Hawick and Carlisle?

49   In which year did the 10.00am Scotch express from King's Cross acquire the name *Flying Scotsman?*

50   Which railway company came to the rescue of the Metropolitan Railway with the loan of locomotives and rolling stock after the Great Western Railway unilaterally withdrew from a working agreement in 1863?

51   The acquisition of which ancient railway, originally built as a tramroad in 1802, gave the London & North Western Railway access to Newport, Monmouthshire, in 1875?

52   On what date did the Midland and London & South Western railways jointly take over the Somerset & Dorset Railway on a 999 year lease?

53   When did the Bristol & Exeter and Great Western railways amalgamate?

54   When was the Settle and Carlisle line of the Midland Railway opened for all traffic?

55   What was the date of the Abbots Ripton accident on the Great Northern Railway, which had far-reaching effects on British signalling practice?

56   Which large concern acquired control of the Corris Railway in 1878?

57   Which railway first introduced proper dining cars into Great Britain in 1879?

58   Who was the driving force behind the Barry Railway & Docks Co, prophesying that he would 'make grass grow in the streets of Cardiff'?

59   Who owned the line, worked by the Highland Railway, between Golspie and Helmsdale from 1871–84?

60   Who was the chairman of the London, Chatham & Dover and Metropolitan District railways and the great business rival of Sir Edward Watkin of the Great Central and Metropolitan railways?

61   Where was the southerly extremity of the lengthy Great Northern & Great Eastern Joint line, the most northerly point of which was Black Carr Junction, south of Doncaster?

62   In which year was the Management Committee set up that effectively amalgamated the South Eastern and the London, Chatham & Dover railways, although both retained a separate legal existence?

63   Which three railway companies were partners in the Cheshire Lines Committee?

64   Who served the Rhymney Railway for forty-six years as engineer, traffic manager and general manager?

65   Who was appointed general manager of the Lancashire & Yorkshire Railway in June 1899?

66   What was unique about the ownership of Aylesbury Town station, Buckinghamshire?

67   Who was general manager of the Midland & South Western Junction Railway between 1892–9 and later went on to serve in the same capacity for a larger railway and to earn a knighthood?

68   Which was the first British railway to operate motor bus services in connection with rail services?

69   Which two companies were partners in operating the Taff Bargoed Railway?

70   Who retired as general manager of the London & North Western Railway in 1909?

71   Which two companies prior to 1923 were partners in the Axholme Joint Railway in the wilds of north Lincolnshire?

72   On what date did the Great Western Railway take over operation of the South Wales Mineral Railway?

73   When did the Harwich-Zeebrugge train ferry commence regular operation?

74   When were regular passenger services between Cuffley and Hertford North inaugurated by the London & North Eastern Railway?

75   What was the full title of the light railway between Chichester and Selsey, part of the Col Stephens' empire, which closed completely in 1935?

76   What caused the premature closure of the Jersey Railway in 1936?

77   On what date did the London & North Eastern Railway assume total control of the Midland & Great Northern Railway?

78   In what year was the Railway Executive abolished, its

functions being transferred to the British Transport Commission?

79   What was the name of the former London & North Western Railway terminus in Bolton, closed to passengers in 1954?

80   When was the much-vaunted British Railways' 'Modernisation Plan', which resulted in the destruction of so much equipment and saddled the railways with crippling capital debts, first announced?

81   Which English railway was the first to introduce Pullman cars, in 1874?

82   Which two companies combined in 1850 to form the Glasgow & South Western Railway?

83   In which year did the 'Battle of Havant' take place between gangs of platelayers and navvies from the London & South Western and London, Brighton & South Coast railways over the question of access to Portsmouth?

84   What name was given to the Pullman train introduced on the London, Brighton & South Coast Railway in 1888?

85   Where in London did the South Eastern Railway open a city terminus in 1866?

86   Which pre-grouping railway company owned the largest number of steamships?

87   Where in Great Britain was the Golden Valley Railway, opened throughout on 27 May 1889?

88   In which year was the contract signed for the carriage of Royal Mail by the Great Eastern Railway's steamships between Harwich and Rotterdam?

89   In what year did the London, Chatham & Dover Railway find itself in Chancery, due to chronic financial problems?

90   From which railway did Charles Scotter come to the London & South Western Railway as general manager in 1885?

91 The projected amalgamation of which three large British railway companies was vetoed by Parliament in 1908?

92 What was the name by which the East Kent Railway became known in 1859?

93 Which two companies operated the Portpatrick & Wigtownshire Joint Railway from Castle Douglas to Stranraer?

94 Which railway company lost heavily in the 1881 failure of the Sutton Bridge Dock Co?

95 Which railway company operated the services on the Invergarry & Fort Augustus Railway, between Spean Bridge and Fort Augustus, from 27 July 1903 until 31 October 1911?

96 What was the destination of the 'American Special' trains operated from Euston by the London & North Western Railway?

97 Apart from the Great Western Railway, which two companies participated in the tripartite amalgamation of 1863, forming the bulk of the expanded Great Western system?

98 Who became chairman of the Great Western Railway in 1861?

99 In 1846 two railways were absorbed by the Midland Railway. One was the Birmingham & Gloucester; which was the other?

100 Which Welsh railway was acquired by the Midland Railway in 1874, giving the Midland circuitous access to Swansea?

101 Which old-established railway amalgamated with the North Eastern Railway in 1862?

102 When was the opening of the present station at York, designed by Thomas Prosser, Benjamin Burley and William Peachey and which replaced the original terminus within the city walls?

103   Between which two places in northern England was a broad gauge atmospheric railway projected in 1845?

104   Which former London terminus finally closed to freight traffic after a disastrous fire on 5 December 1964?

105   In what year did the Great Western Railway reach Oxford, from the junction on the original main line at Didcot?

106   Who was chairman of the London & North Western Railway until succeeded in 1891 by Lord Stalbridge?

107   In what year did the Midland Railway acquire the Belfast & Northern Counties Railway?

108   When did the first section of the Victoria Line open, between Walthamstow Central and Highbury & Islington?

109   In what year did the Lancaster & Carlisle Railway absorb the Lancaster & Preston Railway?

110   In what year was the South Devon Railway constrained to purchase its own locomotive stock after its working agreement with the Great Western Railway expired?

111   What was carried on the 'Jellicoe Specials' during World War I?

112   When did the *Golden Arrow* make its last run from Victoria to Dover?

113   Despite the completion of a junction with the Taff Vale Railway at Treforest, what was the furthest point from Cardiff ever reached by the passenger services of the Cardiff Railway?

114   In what year did the London & North Western Railway acquire the whole of its route from Euston to Carlisle, by taking a lease on the Lancaster & Carlisle Railway?

115   The South Wales Railway from Chepstow to Swansea was completed and opened in 1851. Why was through running from Gloucester delayed a further year?

116   In which year did the London & North Western and Great Western railways jointly take over the Birkenhead Railway?

117   To take up what government appointment did Lord Cawdor resign the chairmanship of the Great Western Railway?

118   Which Manchester terminus was originally used by Midland Railway trains from Derby via Matlock and Chinley?

119   In what year did Sir James Allport announce that henceforth the Midland Railway would carry third-class passengers by all trains?

120   Who organised his first excursion from Leicester to Loughborough and back on the Midland Counties Railway, for a fare of one shilling, in 1840?

121   Who succeeded George Hudson as chairman of the Midland Railway after his disgrace?

122   In what year did the North Eastern Railway push south from York through Selby, to meet the Great Northern Railway 'in a ploughed field near Shaftholme'?

123   From 1857 where did the Great Northern Railway hand over its 'Manchester Flyer' trains to the Manchester, Sheffield & Lincolnshire Railway, to be hauled thence to Manchester London Road?

124   In what year was the great amalgamation of East Anglian railways that produced the Great Eastern Railway?

125   Where in Manchester was the original terminus of the Manchester & Leeds Railway, replaced as inadequate by the new Victoria station at Hunts Bank in 1844?

126   What small independent railway was acquired by the Great Central Railway in 1905?

127   What title was taken by Sir Alexander Henderson, chairman of the Great Central Railway, on his elevation to the House of Lords?

128   Between which two points on the Metropolitan Railway was the Great Central Railway granted running powers under its 1893 Act of Parliament?

129   In which year did the Cornwall Railway reach Truro and meet the standard gauge West Cornwall Railway?

130   In which year did the London & North Western Railway take over responsibility for the working of the North London Railway?

PRIZE QUESTIONS
British Railway History
(indicate the correct answer on the entry form on page 131)

Q1 Who was the first chairman of the London & North Eastern Railway from 1923?

A Sir Ronald Matthews.
B Sir Murrough Wilson.
C Andrew K. McCosh.
D William Whitelaw.

Q2 Which Act of Parliament compelled the grouping of the railway companies into the 'Big Four' in 1923?

A The Transport Act, 1920.
B The Railways Act, 1921.
C The Railways Act, 1922
D The Transport Act, 1921.

Q3 Of which English railway did the American Henry Thornton (later Sir Henry) become general manager in 1914?

A Great Northern Railway.
B Great Central Railway.
C Great Eastern Railway.
D South Eastern & Chatham Railway.

Q4 Who was chairman of the Great Western Railway from 1908–34?

A Sir Felix Pole.
B Viscount Churchill.
C Sir James Milne.
D Sir Josiah Stamp.

Q5 In what year did the Manchester, Sheffield & Lincolnshire Railway assume the title 'Great Central Railway'?

A 1894.
B 1896.
C 1897.
D 1899.

Q6   In which two years of the late nineteenth century did the famous, if unofficial, 'Race to the North' take place between the East Coast and the West Coast companies for the Scottish holiday traffic?

A   1888 and 1892.
B   1886 and 1892.
C   1892 and 1895.
D   1888 and 1895.

Q7   On what date did the first passenger train work into Waterloo station in London?

A   3 July 1847.
B   13 July 1848.
C   13 June 1848.
D   13 July 1847.

Q8   Which eminent Victorian contractor was awarded the contract to build the main line of the Great Northern Railway between King's Cross and Peterborough?

A   Thomas Brassey.
B   Samuel Morton Peto.
C   John Scott Russell.
D   John Urpeth Rastrick.

Q9   Which West Country town was reached by the London & South Western Railway with the opening for traffic of the circuitous line known as 'Castleman's Snake' on 7 June 1847?

A   Salisbury.
B   Dorchester.
C   Wimborne.
D   Weymouth.

Q10   What title did the London & York Railway assume before obtaining its Act of Parliament in 1846?

A   Great North of England Railway.
B   London & Midland Counties Railway.
C   Great Northern Railway.
D   Direct Northern Railway.

Q11   On what date did traffic cease on the horse-worked Surrey Iron Railway, the first public goods-carrying railway to be authorised by Act of Parliament?

A 31 August 1844.
B 31 August 1846.
C 31 August 1848.
D 31 August 1850.

Q12 On what date did the Midland Counties Railway, the North Midland Railway and the Birmingham & Derby Junction Railway amalgamate to form the Midland Railway?

A 14 May 1844.
B 10 May 1844.
C 5 June 1844.
D 9 July 1844.

Q13 On what date was the Railway Clearing House established in London to handle inter-company revenue accounts?

A 2 January 1846.
B 2 January 1852.
C 2 January 1842.
D 2 January 1844.

Q14 Where in Edinburgh was the original terminus of the Edinburgh & Glasgow Railway in 1841?

A Dalry Road.
B Murrayfield.
C Haymarket.
D Gorgie.

Q15 What trade was followed by George Hudson of York before turning to railway speculation?

A Butcher.
B Banker.
C Fishmonger.
D Draper.

Q16 On what date did the Grand Junction Railway open throughout from Curzon Street, Birmingham, to the junction with the Liverpool & Manchester Railway at Warrington?

A 4 April 1837.
B 4 May 1837.
C 4 June 1837.
D 4 July 1837.

Q17 When was the public opening of the first section of the London & Greenwich Railway, from Spa Road, Bermondsey, to Deptford?

A 8 February 1836.
B 8 March 1836.
C 8 April 1836.
D 8 May 1836.

Q18 Where was it originally intended that the London & Birmingham Railway should terminate in London, the extension to Euston not being authorised until 3 July 1835?

A Primrose Hill.
B Chalk Farm.
C Camden Town.
D Paddington.

Q19 What was the date of the circular letter sent out by John Cave calling the first meeting of interested parties to discuss the building of a railway from Bristol to London?

A 4 April 1833.
B 16 March 1833.
C 21 January 1833.
D 9 February 1833.

Q20 At the time of the opening of the Stockton & Darlington Railway in 1825, who was chairman of the company?

A Thomas Meynell of Yarm.
B Edward Pease of Darlington.
C George Stephenson.
D John Rennie.

British Railway Engineering

answers on pp 110-113

1 Who was the master mason who built the Tanfield or Causey (Causeway) Arch, the world's first major railway bridge, on the Tanfield Wagonway in 1727?

2 What is the distance spanned by the Tanfield Arch on the Tanfield Wagonway in County Durham?

3 What is the name of the great bog crossed by the Liverpool & Manchester Railway west of Eccles?

4 Who was appointed as chief engineer of the London & Southampton in place of the original engineer, Francis Giles, who proved totally incompetent?

5 After whom was the viaduct on the Great Western Railway between Hanwell and Southall named?

6 Approximately how many bricks were calculated to have been incorporated in the lining of Kilsby Tunnel on the London & Birmingham Railway?

7 Who was the architect who designed the Doric portico and Great Hall at Euston station, so tragically demolished in the 1960s?

8 Where on the London & Birmingham Railway is the great cutting through the Chiltern Hills?

9 Between which two points did the Great Western Railway install Cooke & Wheatstone's electric telegraph in 1839?

10 To what gauge were the first sections of the Eastern Counties Railway (Bishopsgate to Romford and Stratford to Bishop's Stortford) originally built?

11 Who became engineer of the London & York Railway in 1844, following the resignation of Joseph Locke?

12 Which great railway bridge was formally opened by Queen Victoria on 1 August 1850?

13   On which building did Lewis Cubitt base his design for the roof span of King's Cross station?

14   How many tunnels were and are there on the Great Northern Railway between King's Cross and Hitchin?

15   What was the major civil engineering feature of the Cornwall Railway?

16   Where did the Midland & Great Northern Railway have its locomotive workshops until their closure for all but minor repairs in December 1936?

17   Where was the first set of water troughs out of King's Cross on the Great Northern Railway main line?

18   What is the longest tunnel on the Southern Region?

19   Where did Sir Edward Watkin commence the construction of a tower to rival the Eiffel Tower in Paris?

20   What was the name of the viaduct by which the Barry Railway crossed the valley of the River Taff at Taff's Well?

21   Which was the first railway to introduce automatic apparatus for the exchange of tablets at speed on single lines?

22   The construction of which standard gauge railway was supervised by I. K. Brunel simultaneously with the building of the Great Western Railway in 1836–41?

23   Where was the locomotive works of the Brecon & Merthyr Railway?

24   Who designed the viaduct at Cefn, carrying the former Great Western Railway main line over the River Dee?

25   Where were the first water troughs installed by John Ramsbottom on the London & North Western Railway in 1860?

26   Which locomotive engineer invented the automatic tablet exchange apparatus, generously refusing to patent his invention?

27   How much was the prize money offered by the Liverpool & Manchester Railway committee for the most satisfactory locomotive at the Rainhill Trials?

28   What method of traction was recommended for the Liverpool & Manchester Railway in the report submitted by Rastrick and Walker on 9 March 1829?

29   When was Kilsby Tunnel on the London & Birmingham Railway opened to trains?

30   On what date was the meeting of the shareholders of the Stockton & Darlington Railway at which George Stephenson was appointed engineer to the company at a salary of £660pa?

31   For what distance was steam traction employed on the opening of the Canterbury & Whitstable Railway in 1830?

32   What is the height above sea level of Druimuachdar Summit on the main line of the former Highland Railway?

33   Where was the steepest gradient over which standard gauge passenger trains were worked in Great Britain?

34   Where was it first proposed to install Cooke & Wheatstone's electric telegraph on a railway, the idea being abandoned before the telegraph could be installed?

35   How long is Bramhope Tunnel near Harrogate on the former Leeds Northern Railway?

36   Of what material was Glenfinnan Viaduct on the Mallaig extension of the former North British Railway constructed?

37   Where in Great Britain was the Bennie rail-plane, an aerial, airscrew-driven monorail affair, briefly demonstrated in the mid-1930s?

38   What was the original, hopelessly underestimated contract price for the construction of Kilsby Tunnel on the London & Birmingham Railway?

39   What is the maximum height of Meldon Viaduct, near Okehampton, on the former London & South

Western Railway?

40   What was the purpose of the Coligny-Welch reflector, as used on certain signal lamps by a few British railways, particularly the London, Brighton & South Coast?

41   The overall roof of which London terminus collapsed in December 1905?

42   Which part of the white cliffs of Dover was dynamited out of the route of the South Eastern Railway by William Cubitt, in consultation with Lt Hutchinson RE, on 26 January 1843?

43   How long is Ponsbourne Tunnel, situated between Cuffley and Hertford stations, on the former Great Northern Railway?

44   When did the 'other' Forth Bridge open between Throsk and Alloa on the Caledonian Railway?

45   In the Wormit foundry set up to supply castings for the first Tay Bridge, what was the name given to the paint-like concoction applied to the castings to conceal poor workmanship?

46   What area of water is crossed by the two viaducts between Quorn and Rothley on the London Extension of the Great Central Railway?

47   How was the incline at Beck Hole on the Whitby & Pickering Railway worked before the installation of a stationary steam engine?

48   When did construction of the Victoria Bridge over the River Severn at Arley on the Severn Valley Railway commence with the laying of the foundation stone?

49   In what year did Charles Tayleur found the Vulcan Foundry at Newton-le-Willows, later to build some of the first locomotives for the Great Western Railway?

50   At its maximum extent, what area was covered by Swindon works?

51   Of what material did Thomas Bouch build Hownes Gill Viaduct near Consett, Co Durham, on the Stockton &

Darlington Railway?

52 In what year did the Midland Railway open its new port and harbour complex at Heysham for the Irish traffic?

53 Where did the Great North of Scotland Railway open a new locomotive works in 1903, replacing the earlier establishment at Kittybrewster, Aberdeen?

54 Which tunnel on the London & North Western Railway had water troughs laid inside it?

55 Which was the last line in Great Britain to be built and operated on Brunel's 7ft gauge?

56 Which was the first large section of the Great Western Railway to be converted from broad to standard gauge, in 1868?

57 At the time of the absorption into the Great Western Railway on 10 September 1922, who was chief engineer of the Cardiff Railway?

58 What waterway was crossed by the swinging span of the Severn Bridge, on the line between Sharpness and Lydney in Gloucestershire?

59 What river is crossed by the London & Birmingham Railway viaduct near Wolverton?

60 Where was the locomotive works of the West Cornwall Railway prior to 1865?

61 Where was the first mechanical locomotive coaling plant built in Great Britain, in 1913?

62 How long is Greenock Tunnel on the former Caledonian Railway, the longest railway tunnel in Scotland?

63 Who designed the roof span of St Pancras station for the Midland Railway?

64 Who was the originator of the railway swing bridge, the first being built at Reedham on the Norwich & Lowestoft Railway?

65 Who designed Connell Ferry cantilever bridge to carry the Ballachulish branch of the Caledonian Railway across the mouth of Loch Etive?

66 Whose resignation caused the locomotive affairs of the North Eastern Railway to be managed by a committee headed by Henry Tennant, the general manager, in 1884–5?

67 Which was the only British railway to continue to roll rails in its own rolling mill into the twentieth century?

68 How many spans has Templand Viaduct, near Old Cumnock on the former Glasgow & South Western Railway?

69 Where was the workshop of the Eastern Counties Railway prior to the establishment of the first works at Stratford in 1847?

70 Who was the civil engineer who constructed the Highland Railway main line over Druimuachdar Summit in 1845–63?

71 Which two engineers were knighted on completion of the Mersey Railway tunnel from Liverpool to Birkenhead in 1886?

72 In what year was the first recognisable signal-box erected in Britain, at Corbett's Lane Junction, Southwark, on the London & Greenwich Railway?

73 Who was the architect of the Moorish arch at Edge Hill, Liverpool, on the Liverpool & Manchester Railway?

74 What was the weight of each truss of Brunel's Royal Albert Bridge at Saltash when first constructed?

75 Where, in the summer of 1875, did trials take place under Board of Trade auspices between various systems of train braking, the automatic vacuum and Westinghouse systems emerging as clearly superior?

76 Where was the highest railway tunnel in Great Britain?

77 Who was the carriage and wagon superintendent of

the London & North Western Railway who designed the Royal Train for King Edward VII and Queen Alexandra in 1902–3?

78   What was the most spectacular engineering feature of the Lynton & Barnstaple Railway?

79   Where was the locomotive building works of the London & South Western Railway prior to 1910?

80   In what year did cable operation of the incline from Euston to Camden Town cease on the London & Birmingham Railway?

PRIZE QUESTIONS
British Railway Engineering
(*indicate the correct answer on the entry form on page 132*)

Q1 In what year were cast-iron flanged wheels for tramway wagons first cast at Coalbrookdale in Shropshire?

A 1729.
B 1739.
C 1749.
D 1759.

Q2 Who was the famous civil engineer who designed the 'fish-belly' cast-iron rail for use on tramroads from c1790?

A James Brindley.
B Marc Brunel.
C William Jessop.
D Thomas Telford.

Q3 Which was the first railway to use wrought-iron rails, from c1808?

A The Middleton Railway.
B The Brampton Railway.
C The Surrey Iron Railway.
D The Monmouthshire Tramroad.

Q4 Of what material were the 'rails' of the Haytor Tramway on Dartmoor made?

A Wood.
B Cast iron.
C Granite.
D Wrought iron.

Q5 Which river was spanned by the world's first iron railway bridge, erected at West Auckland by the Stockton & Darlington Railway in 1825?

A River Tyne.
B River Gaunless.
C River Wear.
D River Tees.

Q6 How wide is the central span of the Ballochmyle

Viaduct over the River Ayr on the former Glasgow & South Western Railway?

A   180ft.
B   181ft.
C   182ft.
D   183ft.

Q7   In what year did the Grand Junction Railway move its locomotive works from Edge Hill, Liverpool, to Crewe?

A   1841.
B   1842.
C   1843.
D   1844.

Q8   When was the first bore of Woodhead Tunnel on the line between Manchester and Sheffield opened for traffic?

A   23 December 1844.
B   23 December 1845.
C   23 December 1846.
D   23 December 1847.

Q9   When did atmospheric traction commence on the South Devon Railway between Exeter and Teignmouth?

A   13 June 1847.
B   13 August 1847.
C   13 September 1847.
D   13 July 1847.

Q10   The Doncaster works of the Great Northern Railway was set up by Archibald Sturrock in 1853. Where had the locomotive works been situated prior to 1853?

A   Boston.
B   Grantham.
C   Peterborough.
D   Newark.

Q11   What was the longest railway bridge in Europe prior to the construction of the first Tay Bridge?

A   The Solway Viaduct, Solway Junction Railway.
B   Ballochmyle Viaduct, Glasgow & South Western Railway.
C   Welwyn Viaduct, Great Northern Railway.
D   Harringworth Viaduct, Midland Railway.

Q12 Who was appointed as consulting engineer to the Severn Tunnel project by the Great Western Railway?

A John Fowler.
B Sir Thomas Bouch.
C Sir John Hawkshaw.
D Benjamin Baker.

Q13 How far did the 'High Girders' of the Tay Bridge, which collapsed on 28 December 1879, extend?

A From pier 41 to pier 28.
B From pier 40 to pier 20.
C From pier 41 to pier 30.
D From pier 38 to pier 18.

Q14 Which firm secured the contract for the construction of the Forth Bridge in 1882?

A R. &. W. Hawthorn-Leslie & Co.
B T. A. Walker & Co.
C Sir Robert McAlpine & Co.
D Tancred, Arrol & Co.

Q15 How high was Thomas Bouch's Belah Viaduct in Westmorland, on the former South Durham & Lancashire Union line of the Stockton & Darlington Railway?

A 166ft.
B 176ft.
C 186ft.
D 196ft.

Q16 In which year did the Great Central Railway commence construction of the new dock complex at Immingham in Lincolnshire?

A 1904.
B 1905.
C 1906.
D 1907.

Q17 At which London underground station were escalators first brought into use on 4 October 1911?

A South Kensington.
B Sloane Square.
C Earls Court.
D Down Street.

Q18 On what date was the King George V graving dock at Southampton, built by the Southern Railway, opened by HM King George V?

A 4 July 1933.
B 12 July 1933.
C 20 July 1933.
D 26 July 1933.

Q19 In which year was the Ocean Terminal at Southampton Docks, owned by the Southern Railway and later British Railways, completed?

A 1947.
B 1949.
C 1950.
D 1952.

Q20 Which British mechanical signal-box held the record number of levers in a single frame, with 240 levers, until replaced in 1951?

A Reading West Junction, Great Western Railway.
B Locomotive Yard, York, London & North Eastern Railway.
C London Bridge No 1, Southern Railway.
D Crewe Goods No 1, London Midland & Scottish Railway.

Foreign Railways

answers on pp 114-119

1 Which was the first service to be operated by the Compagnie Internationale des Wagons-Lits?

2 When was the Compagnie Internationale des Wagons-Lits constituted in Brussels by George Nagelmackers, with King Leopold II heading the list of subscribers?

3 When did the civil administration take over from the British army the operation of the railways in Palestine and Transjordan?

4 Who was the New York inventor who built the vertical-boilered locomotive *Tom Thumb* for the Baltimore & Ohio Railroad in 1829?

5 What is the longest wholly Swiss rail tunnel and what is its length?

6 What is the gauge of the Kalka-Simla line of the former North Western Railway of India?

7 On 3 July 1850 the Sydney Railway Co began construction of a railway to Parramatta, 14 miles away. How long did it take to complete the line?

8 Which two towns were connected by the first railway in Finland, opened in 1862?

9 Which was the first de Glehn compound locomotive to be built, in 1885?

10 Which were the last Atlantic locomotives to remain in ordinary service in Europe?

11 On 30 January 1925 the carriages of a train on the Letterkenny & Burtonport Extension Railway were literally blown over the parapet of a viaduct by a gale. What was the name of the viaduct?

12 Who built the first locomotive to run in France, on the St Etienne & Lyons Railway in 1829?

13 A Stephenson Planet-type engine was exported to the USA in 1831. On which railroad did it run from 12 November 1831?

14 Two Stephenson Patentee locomotives were supplied to the Belgian government for use on the railway between Brussels and Malines (Mechelen). A third similar engine was built in Belgium. By whom?

15 To which German railway did Robert Stephenson & Co supply a Patentee type locomotive *Der Adler* in 1835?

16 The first railway in Holland opened between Amsterdam and Haarlem in September 1839. What was its gauge?

17 When was the line over the Semmering Pass between Gloggnitz and Mürzzuschlag in Austria completed?

18 Who drove in the last spike at the ceremony to mark the completion of the Canadian Pacific Railway on 7 November 1885?

19 Which was the last former Prussian P8 class 4-6-0 to run in regular service on the Deutsche Bundesbahn on 22 May 1971?

20 On what date did the first *Orient Express* depart from Paris for Vienna and Constantinople?

21 What is the name of the railway terminus on the Scutari (eastern) side of the Bosporus in Istanbul?

22 In what year were CIWL luxury sleeping car services instituted in Egypt between Alexandria, Cairo and Luxor?

23 Where was the first railway in Greece, opened on 10 March 1869?

24 Which Khedive of Egypt entered into negotiations with Robert Stephenson in 1851 for the construction of a railway from Alexandria to Cairo?

25 What is the name of the bridge over the Menam Chao Phraya at Bangkok in Thailand which connects the northern and southern networks of the Royal State Railways?

26   Where are the only spiral tunnels in North America?

27   What is the Trans Europ Express network?

28   Where was the only spiral railway tunnel in Ireland?

29   Which two locomotives met, smokebox to smokebox, at the completion of the Union Pacific and Central Pacific railroads at Promontory Point, Utah, in 1869?

30   Which countries are linked by the Victoria Falls Bridge and which company built it?

31   Where was the main locomotive building and repair works of the Pennsylvania Railroad?

32   What wheel arrangement is denoted by the USA term 'Niagara'?

33   The last steam locomotive to be built by a railroad company in the USA appeared in December 1953. Which engine was it and what was the railroad company?

34   What is the name of the 8 mile long causeway by which the railway reaches the Island of Sylt from the West German mainland at Klanxbull?

35   What is the gauge of the railway that connects Guaqui and La Paz in Bolivia?

36   Which was the last class of steam locomotive to be introduced on the Swedish State Railways?

37   What were the first articulated locomotives to work in the African continent?

38   In which city of the southern USA was there once a famous three-level intersection between the Chesapeake & Ohio, Seaboard Air Line and Southern railroads?

39   When was the new Cascade Tunnel on the Great Northern Railroad, USA, completed and opened for electric trains?

40   Which was the last of the 2ft gauge lines in the state of Maine, USA, to close in December 1944?

41 When did the Key West extension of the Florida East Coast Railroad close following hurricane damage?

42 By what names was the railway system of the Irish Republic known from 1 January 1925 until the Eire Transport Act of 1944 set up the present administration, Coras Iompair Eireann?

43 What was unusual about the Steffenbach bridge on the Furka-Oberalp Railway in Switzerland?

44 By what nickname was the Norfolk & Western Railroad's steam-turbine electric locomotive, No 2300, generally known?

45 Where are the locomotive works of the Sudan Railways?

46 On which African station was placed the carriage in which an engineer was killed by a man-eating lion?

47 Which railway administration owns the fleet of ships that ply Lake Titicaca in the Andes?

48 Which three major American locomotive builders constructed 141R class 2-8-2s for the SNCF?

49 How many 141R class 2-8-2s were built in the USA and Canada for the SNCF between 1945 and 1947?

50 What is the name of the 5,370ft long steel viaduct by which the Canadian Pacific Railway crosses the Belly River in Alberta?

51 What was the title of the novel by John Masters which is set in a major Indian railway junction?

52 Which French company operated the railway between Liège and Namur on payment to the Belgian government of an annual rent?

53 Which route linking railways in northern Europe and Italy was opened in 1882?

54 What nickname was given to the four-cylinder Maffei 4-6-0s of the Netherlands Central Railway, introduced in 1910?

55   Which country in Africa used standard gauge (4ft 8½in) Garratt locomotives, the prototype of which was tried out in France?

56   Which two narrow gauge sections of the Denver & Rio Grande Railroad are still open for tourist steam-worked trains?

57   Which two railways were connected by the 80½km North Brabant German Railway?

58   When did railway services between Belfast and Dublin commence with the completion of the viaduct over the Boyne at Drogheda?

59   For which railroad did the American Locomotive Co build four oil-fired streamlined Atlantics as late as 1935?

60   What is the gauge of the Russian railway system?

61   Around the Indian National Railway Museum in Delhi is a steam-worked monorail system. In which state of the Punjab was this equipment used between 1907–27, thereafter lying derelict for almost fifty years?

62   When did the 5,248ft long bridge over the Yangtze Kiang river between Nanking and Pukow open for traffic, replacing the train ferry that had operated since 1933?

63   What name was carried by the first locomotive to operate in Argentina, an 0-4-0ST built in Leeds in 1857?

64   Which was the first railway to be built in Turkey using entirely Turkish capital and labour, being inaugurated on 22 September 1924?

65   Which small Irish railway was formerly wholly owned by the London & North Western Railway?

66   What was the first stretch of the Paris Metro to open, in 1900?

67   What was the original gauge of the Louisville & Nashville Railroad in the USA?

68   In what year did the first portion of the New York elevated railroad, or 'L', open with steam traction?

69   In which country is a remarkable section of zig-zag railway up a mountain named the 'Devil's Nose'?

70   Which British 4-6-0 design was used as the basis for a batch of fifty engines supplied to French State Railways in 1911?

71   What was the gauge of the projected railway that Hitler intended to build from Germany to Russia for the provision of troops?

72   On what date was the *Flèche d'Or*, the French half of the *Golden Arrow*, last steam hauled between Amiens and Calais?

73   What was the last year of regular steam operation on the Belgian State Railways?

74   Of which Continental railway was James Staats Forbes general manager in the nineteenth century?

75   The Canadian Pacific Railway class H1c, H1d and H1e 4-6-4s Nos 2820-64 were known as Royal Hudsons. How did they acquire this distinction and what decorative feature was applied to them?

76   Which Italian signal engineer had a considerable hand in designing the block instruments and signalling on the Great Western Railway?

77   For which service did S. E. Haagsma, chief mechanical engineer of the Dutch State Railway, order five large outside-frame Atlantics from Beyer Peacock & Co in 1900?

78   In which country would one find railways negotiating the Bolan and Khojak passes?

79   Who designed the class of large four-cylinder Pacifics built for the Belgian State Railways from 1910?

80   In what year did non-stop expresses commence between Paris and Brussels?

81   Which Austrian private railway continued to operate former Austrian Sudbahn 29 class 0-6-0 locomotives, built in 1860, until at least 1969?

82   What are defined by the Interstate Commerce Commission in the USA as 'Class 1 Railroads'?

83   What is the name of the 5 mile tunnel in British Columbia which replaces the original steeply graded route of the Canadian Pacific Railway over Rogers Pass in the Selkirk Mountains?

84   Which was the first railway to connect the Atlantic Ocean with the Pacific, opened on 28 January 1855?

85   On what date was the through standard gauge route from Perth to Sydney completed with the conversion of the Port Pirie to Broken Hill section?

86   Which river is crossed by the Thomas Viaduct, the oldest stone viaduct in the USA, carrying the Washington branch of the Baltimore & Ohio Railroad?

87   Where is the most southerly railway in the world?

88   When did the first transalpine railway open through the Brenner Pass between Austria and Italy?

89   How long is the dead straight stretch of the Australian Port Augusta to Kalgoorlie line across the Nullarbor Plain?

90   The Trans-Siberian Railway was not completed on purely Russian soil until 1916. From 1901–16, over which railway was trans-Siberian traffic worked through Manchuria to Vladivostock?

91   Who was the American engineer who built the Central Railway of Peru and several other spectacular railways in South America?

92   Where is the world's steepest rack railway?

93   How many platforms, all below ground level, does Grand Central station in New York possess?

94   Where were the main workshops of the Norfolk & Western Railroad?

95   The Deutsche Reichsbahn was set up on 1 April 1920. In what year was an Act passed by the Reichstag

making the Reichsbahn administration independent of the government?

96 Which was the first section of the Chemin de Fer Paris-Orléans main line to be electrified at 1500 volts DC, the installation coming into use in December 1926?

97 Who was the engineer who oversaw the construction of the railway from Genoa to Turin for the Sardinian government?

98 Where did the standard gauge railway from Sydney meet the 5ft 3in gauge railway from Melbourne, at the New South Wales/Victoria border, on 14 June 1888?

99 The South African *Blue Train* from Cape Town to Johannesburg was re-equipped with new rolling stock in 1972. To which service was the original *Blue Train* stock transferred?

100 What title was imposed on the formerly British-owned Buenos Aires Great Southern Railway following nationalisation of the Argentine railways by the Perón regime?

101 Whose name has been given to the 4 mile 705yd long bridge carrying the New Orleans Public Belt Railroad over the Mississippi River north of New Orleans?

102 What does the abbreviation 'BART' stand for in connection with the San Francisco underground railway system?

103 What was the name of the famous 1 in 15 incline worked on the Fell centre rail system between Wellington and Masterton in New Zealand?

104 What was the name of the train run by the Pennsylvania Railroad as a direct rival to the New York Central's *Twentieth Century Limited* between New York and Chicago?

105 The name of which Scottish engineer has been given to the type of articulated engine which he was instrumental in developing? His ideas were expounded in a pamphlet published in 1864, and the majority of such locomotives were built for overseas railways, although

examples were constructed for several minor railways and for the Festiniog Railway.

106   Which two American cities were connected by the luxurious *Crescent Limited* train, first run in 1925 and operated jointly by the Pennsylvania, the Louisville & Nashville and the Southern railroads?

107   What political threat caused the British government to finance and guarantee the construction of the Canadian Pacific Railway?

108   Which alpine pass was crossed by a narrow gauge railway working on the Fell centre-rail braking system, pending completion of a tunnel through the mountains?

109   In which single year did the *Golden Mountain Pullman* train operate over the Montreux-Oberland Railway?

110   Which railway company obtained in 1912 a concession to operate eight specially built observation cars between Vienna and Zurich and Vienna and Trieste?

111   What name was given to the express train inaugurated in 1925 by the Compagnie Internationale des Wagons-Lits to connect Istanbul with Ankara?

112   Which is the only surviving railway terminus in West Berlin?

113   What is the name given to the bridge over the Rhine immediately east of the main station at Cologne?

114   Which railway in Africa took delivery of a batch of de Glehn four-cylinder compound Atlantics in 1901?

115   What caused the abandonment of development work on the huge four-cylinder compound 4-6-4s on the Northern Railway of France?

116   The twenty de Glehn Pacifics delivered to the Northern Railway of France in 1912 were a direct copy of a de Glehn design of 1909 for which other railway?

117   What was the name of the German sleeping and dining car company set up in 1916, originally with confiscated

CIWL rolling stock?

118   What was the name of the 4½ mile long rail tunnel in Massachusetts, USA, on which construction had started before 1851 but which was not completed until 1875?

119   Who was the engineer responsible for the awe-inspiring Garabit Viaduct in France?

120   In what year was Chicago Union station completed at a cost of 90 million dollars?

121   Who was the American entrepreneur behind the construction of the Florida East Coast Railway, leading directly to the development of eastern Florida as a major resort area?

122   Which country owned the most powerful Beyer Garratt locomotive?

123   What was the original mileage from Omaha to Oakland, California, by the original Union & Central Pacific Railroad, opened throughout in 1869?

124   How many tunnels are there on the Kalka–Simla Railway in India?

125   How high above sea level is the summit of the Darjeeling Himalaya Railway at Ghum, near Darjeeling?

126   What was the name of the light railway that connected Salzburg and Bad Ischl until closure in 1957?

127   What caused the closure of the funicular railway built by Thomas Cooke & Co near Naples in 1880, and celebrated in the song 'Funiculi-Funicular' by Luigi Denza?

128   Which railway terminus has the largest overall roof in South America?

129   Where is the longest station platform on the Indian sub-continent?

130   In what year was the first Pecos High Bridge completed, carrying the Southern Pacific Railroad over the

Pecos River, 219 miles west of San Antonio, Texas?

131   Why was the Uganda Railway built to metre gauge instead of the Cape gauge of 3ft 6in?

132   What was the name and gauge of the railway which Col T. E. Lawrence rendered useless during World War I?

PRIZE QUESTIONS
Foreign Railways

(indicate the correct answer on the entry form on page 132)

Q1 In what year was the first rack railway in Europe, from Vitznau, completed to the summit of the Rigi at Rigi-Kulm, Switzerland?

A 1871.
B 1873.
C 1875.
D 1877.

Q2 Where, in what was then the quasi-independent state of Manchukuo and is now part of China, did the Compagnie Internationale des Wagons-Lits maintain a workshop for the maintenance of its rolling stock?

A Manchuoli.
B Tsitsikhar.
C Mukden.
D Harbin.

Q3 Which British firm built a class of 4-2-2 single-driver express locomotives for the Shanghai–Nanking Railway as late as 1910?

A Kerr Stuart, Stoke.
B Sharp Stewart, Manchester.
C Neilson & Co, Glasgow.
D Beyer Peacock & Co, Manchester.

Q4 Which was the last Indian Railways works to build steam locomotives, the last sixty being built for the metre gauge in 1971?

A Chittaranjan.
B Jamshedpur.
C Jhansi.
D Baroda.

Q5 Which firm built the Dutch four-cylinder 4-6-0 No 3737, now preserved at Utrecht?

A Henschel, Kassel.
B Schwartzkopff, Berlin.
C Werkspoor, Amsterdam.

D Beyer Peacock, Manchester.

Q6 In what year did the first section of the British-owned Benguela Railway, from Lobito to Catumbela, in Portuguese Angola open?

A 1904.
B 1905.
C 1906.
D 1907.

Q7 How long was Little Duck Viaduct, the longest over-sea stretch of the Florida East Coast Railroad's line to Key West, Florida?

A 5 miles.
B 7 miles.
C 9 miles.
D 11 miles.

Q8 In what year did electrical operation of the line from Cape Town to Simonstown in South Africa commence?

A 1927.
B 1928.
C 1929.
D 1930.

Q9 In the southern suburbs of which Dutch city was it occasionally possible to travel by steam tram as late as 1961?

A Utrecht.
B Middelburg.
C Rotterdam.
D Bergen-op-Zoom.

Q10 Which was the last of the Irish 3ft gauge railways to cease operation, in 1961?

A County Donegal Railway.
B Cavan & Leitrim Railway.
C Londonderry & Lough Swilly Railway.
D West Clare Railway.

Q11 Which American railroad built the first Mallet compound, an 0-6-6-0, to run in North America, in 1904?

A Chesapeake & Ohio.
B Baltimore & Ohio.

C Chicago, Burlington & Quincy.
D Union Pacific.

Q12 Where is the French National Railway Museum?

A Mulhouse.
B Paris.
C Lyon.
D Dijon.

Q13 Which American railroad took delivery from Beyer Peacock & Co of a 2-2-2-0 Webb compound, closely based on the London & North Western Railway Teutonic class, in 1888?

A Chesapeake & Ohio.
B Reading.
C Pennsylvania.
D New York Central.

Q14 In what country was Otira Tunnel, the longest tunnel in the British Empire at 5¼ miles?

A India.
B Canada.
C New Zealand.
D Nyasaland.

Q15 Which country does the French TGV (Train Grande Vitesse) run in besides France?

A Switzerland.
B Germany.
C Luxembourg.
D Spain.

Q16 The *Catalan Talgo* TEE between Barcelona and Geneva passes through gauge-changing equipment to alter the wheel sets from 5ft 6in to 4ft 8½in gauge, or vice versa, at which frontier station?

A Cerbère.
B Port Bou.
C Hendaye.
D Ventimiglia.

Q17 In which year was the final section of the railway from Peshawar through the Khyber Pass to Landi Khana, giving through running to just short of the Afghanistan border, opened?

A 1924.
B 1925.
C 1926.
D 1927.

Q18 What are the principal gauges of Australian main line railways?

A 5ft 6in, 3ft 6in, 4ft 8½in.
B 5ft 6in, 4ft 8½in, 3ft.
C 5ft 3in, 4ft 8½in, 1m.
D 5ft 3in, 3ft 6in, 4ft 8½in.

Q19 Where in Java could one see Beyer Peacock-built tram engines running an urban passenger service through the streets until closure in the late 1970s?

A Djakarta.
B Jogjakarta.
C Surabaya.
D Bandung.

Q20 Which British railway sold fifty obsolete 0-6-0 goods engines to the Mediterranean Railway of Italy in 1906?

A London & North Western Railway.
B Great Western Railway.
C Midland Railway.
D North Eastern Railway.

Diesel and Electric Locomotives and Railways

answers on pp 120-121

1   Which was the first British Railways locomotive to appear in rail blue livery, in May 1964?

2   To which foreign administration was the Hawker Siddeley prototype HS4000 *Kestrel* sold, being shipped from Cardiff on 8 July 1971?

3   To which motive power depot were all the Western Region Hymek diesel-hydraulic locomotives delivered prior to February 1962 allocated?

4   On which German type of locomotive was the design of the Western Region Warship class diesel-hydraulic locomotives based?

5   Which British firm built MAN engines under licence from the German manufacturers for use on the Western Region diesel-hydraulic locomotives?

6   Which was the first type 4 diesel locomotive to be handed over to British Railways under the 1955 Modernisation Plan?

7   Which was the first of the Western Region D1000 class to be turned out at Crewe works, in July 1962?

8   What was the British Railways number of the 4-8-4 diesel-mechanical 2,000hp locomotive built by the Fell Locomotive Co which ran on the London Midland Region from 1951?

9   What was the horsepower of the short-lived Paxman-engined 14 class diesel-hydraulic 0-6-0s, numbered D9500-55?

10   What was the final total of Brush type 4 (BR class 47) diesel-electric locomotives to be built for British Rail?

11   The English Electric 2,750hp gas turbine, GT3, was

built on a pair of spare frames for which class of steam locomotive?

12   What was the number and name of the Birmingham Railway Carriage & Wagon Co prototype locomotive on which the design of the Brush type 4 (class 47) locomotive was largely based?

13   Which was the first ac electric locomotive to run on British Railways, in 1958?

14   Which British Rail works carried out a programme of refurbishment on the London Midland Region 25kV ac class AL4 (later class 84) locomotives between 1970–2?

15   Which foreign railway was the recipient of the first post-war export order for British 25kV ac locomotives in 1968–9?

16   Which was the first thyristor-controlled ac locomotive to be built for British Rail at Crewe in 1975?

17   Which foreign railway bought a batch of 2,580hp locomotives from Brush of Loughborough in 1965, virtually identical with British Rail's class 47?

18   On completion of the electrification between Manchester, Liverpool and Euston, which was the first passenger train to be electrically hauled out of Euston?

19   What was the maximum speed achieved by the French Co-Co electric locomotive No 7107 between Facture and Morcenx on the Bordeaux–Hendaye line on 28 March 1955?

20   On what date was the electrically hauled passenger service between Manchester Piccadilly and Sheffield Victoria via Woodhead Tunnel withdrawn?

21   Which London Midland Region class AL1 25kV electric locomotive was damaged beyond repair in the Hixon accident on 6 January 1968?

22   Which was the first railway in the world to be electrified using hydro-electric power?

23   What was the maximum extent of electrification at

1,500V dc on the lines from Liverpool Street to the east before conversion to the standard 25kV ac electrification system?

24   Where did Werner von Siemens build the world's first practical electric railway in 1879?

25   When did the recently abandoned APT project first commence track trials on British Rail?

26   What type of former Southern Railway electric multiple units were coloquially known as 'Nelsons'?

27   Which of the Southern Railway's 5-BEL electric all-Pullman units for the *Brighton Belle* service was severely damaged in an air raid at Victoria station on 9 October 1940?

28   In what year did the first section of the Liverpool Overhead Railway open for traffic?

29   What is the most powerful standard gauge, single-unit electric locomotive in the world?

30   What was the name of the first class 55 Deltic?

31   Just before nationalisation, the London Midland & Scottish Railway and the Southern Railway were building prototype main line diesel-electric locomotives. The Great Western Railway had also commissioned an internal combustion locomotive; what form of power plant was employed and which company built the first locomotive?

32   Which companies collaborated to produce the prototype Co-Co diesel-electric locomotive *Lion*?

33   When was the world's first oil-engined locomotive placed in service and how was it equipped?

34   Which country holds the world speed record for diesel traction?

35   Which motor car manufacturer in Britain had its own fleet of Bo-Bo diesel-electric shunters?

36   Which railway in London had the first automated driverless electric trains?

37   In 1956 British Railways conducted experiments with electrification, using industrial frequency on the former Midland Railway Lancaster–Morecambe–Heysham line with rolling stock specially converted from another area. Which railway originally built the trains concerned, where did they run and which manufacturer's equipment was originally fitted?

38   Which country holds the world speed record for electric traction?

39   Which railway in Britain uses road traffic light signs as distant signals?

40   Which country holds the world speed record for gas-turbine traction?

PRIZE QUESTIONS
Diesel and Electric Locomotives and Railways

(indicate the correct answer on the entry form on page 133)

Q1 Which was the first suburban railway in Great Britain to be converted from steam to electric traction and opened for regular traffic?

A Mersey Railway, Liverpool Central–Rock Ferry.
B Lancashire & Yorkshire Railway, Liverpool–Southport.
C North Eastern Railway, North Tyne coastal routes.
D London, Brighton & South Coast Railway, London Bridge–Victoria.

Q2 What voltage was used by the Midland Railway for its electrification between Lancaster, Morecambe and Heysham?

A 1500V dc overhead.
B 6250V ac 50Hz overhead.
C 6600V ac 25Hz overhead.
D 1200V dc third rail.

Q3 The Tyne & Wear Metro at Newcastle includes a considerable amount of automation in train operation. What form does this take?

A Train speed is controlled automatically by the signals.
B Entire system computerised with driverless trains.
C Radio-controlled doors.
D Automatic route settings at junctions initiated by transponders from train.

Q4 What form of traction is used on the Glasgow Subway today?

A Cable haulage.
B 1500V dc overhead electrification.
C 600V dc third-rail electrification.
D Diesel-electric engines on the trains.

Q5 Which former *Brighton Belle* Pullman car now operates in the British section of the Simplon-Orient Express?

A   *Brenda.*
B   *Isis.*
C   *Audrey.*
D   *Phoenix.*

Q6   What type of power plant is installed in British Rail HST 125 power cars?

A   English Electric 16 cylinder 2,700hp engine.
B   Paxman Valenta 2,250hp engine.
C   Sulzer 12 cylinder 2,580hp engine.
D   Napier Deltic engines of 1,650hp.

Q7   Why does the London, Tilbury & Southend route require the use of specific electric multiple units to operate it?

A   Platform length is restricted.
B   Stock must be equipped for dual voltage working 25kV/6.25kV.
C   Restricted clearance through curves at Stepney East.
D   Increased power needed for gradients at Westcliff.

Q8   What was the first urban electric railway in Britain (from its opening)?

A   Liverpool Overhead Railway.
B   Glasgow Subway Railway.
C   Waterloo & City line.
D   Metropolitan Railway.

Q9   What is the most powerful class of diesel locomotive ever owned by British Rail?

A   55.
B   56.
C   50.
D   58.

Q10   *Sir Humphrey Chetham* is the name carried by what item of British Rail rolling stock?

A   Class 50 diesel.
B   HST 125 power car.
C   Class 47 diesel.
D   A car of the *Manchester Pullman.*

Q11   Who built the British Railways diesel Blue Pullman trains?

A British Railways, Derby.
B Cravens Ltd, Sheffield.
C Pullman works, Brighton.
D Metro-Cammell, Saltley.

Q12 What was the unique feature of the British Railways type 2 diesel locomotives built by Metropolitan Vickers in 1958 with 1,200hp Crossley engines numbered D5700-19?

A Streamlined cab fronts.
B Equipped with one six-wheel bogie and one four-wheel bogie, described as a Co-Bo.
C First locomotives designed for 100mph running.
D Fitted with automatic couplers.

Q13 At the time of nationalisation, the London Midland & Scottish Railway had in service or on order four main line diesel locomotives. Three were diesel-electrics; what transmission system was fitted to the fourth, designed by Lt Col Fell?

A Hydraulic drive.
B Water turbine.
C Series of interconnected gearboxes.
D Chain and sprocket.

Q14 Which British locomotive engineer tried a turf-burning locomotive in Ireland before designing diesels for Coras Iompair Eireann?

A E. C. Bredin.
B H. G. Ivatt.
C O. V. S. Bulleid.
D R. A. Riddles.

Q15 Which was the first main line in Britain on which all traffic was worked by electric locomotives?

A North Eastern Railway, Newport–Shildon.
B British Railways, Manchester–Crewe.
C British Railways, Liverpool Street–Shenfield.
D British Railways, Manchester–Sheffield.

Q16 Which was the first British titled train to be worked throughout by electric traction?

A *Golden Arrow*.
B *Brighton Belle*.

C   *Master Cutler.*
D   *Royal Scot.*

Q17   What form of braking is used in British Rail HST 125s?

A   Hydro-kinetic.
B   Disc brakes operated by compressed air.
C   Disc brakes operated magnetically.
D   Magnetic rail brakes.

Q18   Part of the order for British Rail class 56 locomotives was built by BR, the remainder by which overseas locomotive works?

A   Swiss Locomotive works, Winterthur, Switzerland.
B   General Motors, La Grange, USA.
C   Mecanoexportimport, Electroputere works, Bucharest, Roumania.
D   Société Alsthom-Atlantique, Paris, France.

Q19   Which British main line railway built the first fleet of diesel railcars?

A   North Eastern Railway.
B   Midland Railway.
C   London Midland & Scottish Railway.
D   Great Western Railway.

Q20   What was unusual about the design of the diesel engines fitted to the British Rail class 55 Deltic locomotives?

A   The most powerful individual engines fitted to a BR diesel.
B   The Napier engines had the cylinders arranged in triangular form, a design which had given good service in ships.
C   The engines were mounted in triangular form within the locomotive body.
D   The engines were coupled together.

Miscellany

answers on pp 122-127

1 Which was the first preserved steam locomotive to break the British Railways Board ban on steam operations over BR tracks, in 1971?

2 What was the main traffic despatched in bulk train-loads from Ashburton Grove yard, near Finsbury Park, to Ayot?

3 In what four locations did the Great Northern Railway operate hotels?

4 What was peculiar about the 3ft 6in gauge railway operated at Swanscombe Cement Works, Kent, by Associated Portland Cement until about 1928?

5 Which was the last former Midland & Great Northern Railway Joint Railway locomotive to remain in British Railways service?

6 The Delaware, Lackawanna & Western Railroad was the setting for the first film made with a cohesive narrative. It was made in 1903 by Edwin S. Porter and the words of its title became famous in a quite different context. What was the title?

7 Who directed the 1924 film *The Iron Horse* for Fox Studios, recounting the building of the Union Pacific Railroad?

8 Which historic locomotive was used in an eponymous film, starring Buster Keaton, in 1927?

9 What was the name of the film made at the Gaumont-British Studios, Lime Grove, in 1932, the title suggesting that a journey to a European capital was the film's subject?

10 On which part of the Great Western Railway was the 1936 film *The Last Journey* made?

11 Which station on the Basingstoke and Alton section of the Southern Railway appeared as 'Buggleskelly' in the film *Oh! Mr Porter* in 1937?

12   In 1862 the London & North Western Railway took out a lease on a railway company in Wales with three towns in its title. What was its name?

13   Two 14XX class 0-4-2Ts appeared in *The Titfield Thunderbolt* in 1952. The most frequently seen engine was No 1401. Which other engine was 'stolen' by Hugh Griffith and Stanley Holloway?

14   Who was the French author of the novel *La Bête Humaine*, a psychological study of Jacques Lantier, a homicidal engine driver on the Paris–Rouen–Normandy route?

15   For what purpose was N7 0-6-2T No 69614, built at Stratford in 1923, kept specially clean between 1956–60?

16   Which British locomotive builder constructed a 2ft 6in gauge 0-4-2ST for the Indonesian Forestry Commission in 1971?

17   Garganville, a redundant French marshalling yard near Paris on SNCF's Eastern Region, was largely blown up on 31 March 1964. Why?

18   For the summer service of 1929, the Great Western Railway accelerated the *Cheltenham Flyer* to make it the world's fastest service train on start to stop timings. What was its average speed?

19   At the maximum extent of the system, how many steam locomotives were employed on the 18in gauge internal railway at Horwich works on the Lancashire & Yorkshire Railway?

20   Which English minor railway was using one of the London & South Western Railway's royal saloons of 1848 as a first-class carriage as late as the 1930s?

21   On which section of the London Midland & Scottish Railway did a steam turbine locomotive, built by Beyer Peacock & Co to the Swedish Ljüngström patents, briefly operate in 1926?

22   What was the maximum number of London stations to have been simultaneously called 'Shepherd's Bush'?

23   What happened to the Shanghai–Woosung Tramway's track and stock after the Chinese government had completed purchase of the railway from Jardine & Matheson in October 1877?

24   Which novel by A. J. Cronin contains an account of the Tay Bridge disaster of 1879?

25   Who headed the administration that improved the punctuality and smartness of the Italian State Railways out of all recognition from 1908 onwards, a feat usually ascribed by popular myth to Mussolini?

26   From 1887–95 no 2-6-0 tender engine ran on any British railway. Which railway reintroduced the type in 1895?

27   What form of valve gear was used on the London & North Western Railway Precedent class 2-4-0s from 1874, a class that included the preserved No 790 *Hardwicke*?

28   What colour were Brecon & Merthyr Railway locomotives painted before 1914?

29   In what year was Stephenson 2-2-2 *North Star* withdrawn from service by the Great Western Railway?

30   In 1937 the London & North Eastern Railway became responsible for the steam motive power of a section of London Transport, taking over the ex-Metropolitan G, H and K class locomotives. Which section of LT?

31   Which was the 7,000th locomotive to be built at Crewe?

32   What conversion was carried out on third-class Pullman cars Nos 13 and 14 by the Pullman car works, Brighton, in 1947?

33   Where was the locomotive hire and repair establishment of Isaac Watt Boulton, immortalised in Rosling Bennett's *The Chronicles of Boulton's Siding*?

34   For five months in 1933 the London Midland & Scottish Railway *Royal Scot* train was exhibited at the 'Century of Progress Exposition'. In which American city was the exhibition held?

35   The Great Northern Railway had twenty 0-4-2 well tanks of Sturrock's design built in Glasgow in 1866. Which other railway took delivery of fourteen almost identical engines at the same time?

36   What private railway crossed the Great Western Railway main line on the level at Laira Junction, Plymouth?

37   The celebrated Welsh bard John Ceiriog Hughes was once general manager of a small railway which had a junction with the Cambrian Railways and was built primarily to carry lead traffic. What was the name of the railway?

38   Which South American country depicted a Great Northern Railway Stirling Single on one of its postage stamps in the 1890s?

39   How was the Stephenson-built *North Star* actually delivered to the Great Western Railway from Newcastle in 1837?

40   Who performed the reopening ceremony for the Dart Valley Railway at Buckfastleigh on 21 May 1969?

41   What was the name of the small 0-4-4T built by Sharp Stewart & Co for the 3rd Duke of Sutherland in 1892 and now preserved in Canada?

42   What was the main colour in which locomotives of the Hull & Barnsley Railway were painted in 1914?

43   Which was the first Pullman car to be operated on a Continental boat train between London and the Kent coast?

44   What indignity was suffered by Stanier Class 5 4-6-0 No 5212 in the course of a filming assignment on the Keighley & Worth Valley Railway in February 1969?

45   For what special duty did the Taff Vale Railway take delivery of three 0-6-0Ts from Kitson & Co (works Nos 2697-9) with sloping firebox crown sheets and deeply coned boilers?

46   For which great opera singer did the Neath & Brecon Railway provide a private waiting room at Craig-y-Nos station?

47   Which great French impressionist painter created a series of canvasses depicting Gare St Lazare, Paris, in the 1870s?

48   What was the last occasion on which a Gresley A4 Pacific worked into King's Cross station?

49   Why were the Flaman speed recorders removed from LNER locomotives after June 1940?

50   Who wrote, in Latin, the book *De Re Metallica*, published in 1556, which contains a treatise on the construction of wooden mine railways?

51   What was the average 'gauge' of the grooved stone wagonways apparently used by the ancient Greeks, remains of which are visible all over Greece?

52   *Hardman* was the name given to the first of which famous class of goods engine designed by John Ramsbottom for the London & North Western Railway in 1858?

53   What locomotive fitting was first marketed by Davies & Metcalfe of Romiley, Cheshire, in 1876?

54   For what purpose did Worsdell S class 4-6-0 No 761, built for the North Eastern Railway in 1906, survive until 1951?

55   On 5 July 1909 the Duchess of Albany performed the opening ceremony of a charitable institution at Woking which has since become well known and which has a miniature railway in the grounds, used to raise money. What is the institution's name?

56   Which was the first class of locomotive designed by Gresley, as opposed to Ivatt designs built under Gresley's superintendency, to be built for the Great Northern Railway in 1912?

57   In what year did Beyer Peacock & Co supply the last of the famous 2-4-0Ts, No 16 *Mannin*, to the Isle of Man Railway?

58   With the building of the deep-level tube railways in London, where did the underground group of companies build a power station to supply the tubes with electricity?

59   Why did the ex-ROD 30XX class 2-8-0s on the Great Western Railway need to be fitted with a special form of Automatic Train Control apparatus?

60   From which company did the Weston, Clevedon & Portishead Light Railway acquire two Sharp Stewart 2-2-2WTs, dating from 1857 and 1866, in 1898-9?

61   Where are the main offices of the Trans Europ Express (TEE) organisation?

62   Which five British Railways Standard 7MT Britannia Pacifics had roller bearings on their driving axles only?

63   Which was the last Gresley A3 Pacific to be built at Doncaster, emerging in February 1935?

64   Where was a locomotive stationary testing plant set up in 1953 on the London Midland Region?

65   How many stations in South Wales bore the name 'Dowlais'?

66   The Gresley A4 Pacific No 4469 *Sir Ralph Wedgwood* was destroyed in an air raid on York in April 1942. To which other A4 was the name transferred in January 1944?

67   Where on the Great Northern Railway of Ireland was there a serious accident on 12 June 1889?

68   Which was the first superheated locomotive to work on a Scottish railway?

69   Where were the last three ex-BR 57XX class pannier tanks on London Transport kept?

70   How old was Bowman Malcolm when he was appointed locomotive engineer of the Northern Counties Railway in Ireland in 1876?

71   In 1893 the first of a long family of engines emerged from Crewe works to the design of F. W. Webb. Its number was 50. What was the class?

72   Which railway company on the Isle of Wight operated all traffic over the Freshwater, Yarmouth & Newport Railway from 1888-1913?

73   When was the King's mail first carried by train in England?

74   What was the furthest point west reached over its own tracks by the Pennsylvania Railroad in the USA?

75   What was carried on the last regular steam-hauled freight trains in Northern Ireland, up to 1969?

76   How many varieties of Dunalastair 4-4-0s of progressively increasing dimensions were built for the Caledonian Railway between 1895 and 1910?

77   A British 0-6-0 goods engine, while serving with the Railway Operating Division in France, was captured by the Germans near Marcoing on 30 November 1917 and used by them until the end of the war. Its number on the British railway was 2717. What was the engine?

78   Bouch 1001 class 0-6-0 No 175 *Contractor* was the first locomotive to be built at which works, in October 1864?

79   Why was much of the day's train service at Paddington disrupted on 2 February 1901?

80   Which railway is promoted as 'The longest preserved line in the world'?

81   Which viaduct, closed in 1921 and dismantled in 1935, was used between those years primarily by Sunday walkers to overcome the licensing laws in the country at one end?

82   Which station on the Liverpool Overhead Railway was actually underground?

83   For which constituency was George Hudson, the 'Railway King', returned as MP in 1845?

84   Which London & North Western Railway Precedent class 2-4-0 is famous for having run in excess of 2 million miles in service, mainly between Euston and Manchester?

85   No 172 *Littlehampton* was the last engine of a famous class to be built, in April 1891. Its best-known sister bore the name of a Victorian Prime Minister. What was the class of engine?

86   In what year did three of the 'Big Four', the exception being the Southern Railway, introduce third-class sleeping cars in Britain?

87   What chemical was contained in the carriage footwarmers introduced on the London & North Western Railway by F. W. Webb in 1880?

88   In the 1895 Race to Scotland, which London & North Western Railway three-cylinder compound Teutonic class 2-2-2-0 covered the 133½ miles from Euston to Stafford in 2 hours 7 minutes?

89   What was the name of the first train ferry to ply between Granton and Burntisland, carrying goods wagons only and built by Robert Napier in 1849?

90   Clapham Junction excepted (most of its acreage consisting of carriage sidings), which British station covered the greatest area prior to the completion of the reconstructed Waterloo in 1922?

91   At what point on the Great Western Railway main line were there two major disasters, one in 1890 and one in 1940?

92   Which was Dugald Drummond's first type of engine design after being appointed locomotive superintendent of the North British Railway in 1875?

93   How many lives were lost during the construction of the Forth Bridge in 1883–90?

94   Who painted the well-known picture *The Railway Station* in 1862, showing Paddington at the zenith of the Great Western Railway's broad gauge era?

95   Which works built all eighty of the British Railways Standard class 4MT 4-6-0s between 1951–7?

96   What was the classic children's story written by E. Nesbit and published in 1906?

97   In what year did London Transport acquire its first ex-BR 57XX class pannier tank?

98   What device was fitted to Battle of Britain class

Pacific No 34064 *Fighter Command*, the only one of the class to be so modified, and for a time to Talyllyn Railway No 4 *Edward Thomas?*

99   Most British Pullman cars were painted in an umber shade with cream upper panels after 1906. What livery was applied to the cars *Mayflower* and *Galatea* which operated over the Metropolitan Railway?

100   Which was the last Atlantic type locomotive to run in ordinary service in the United Kingdom?

101   Which great iron and steel concern made an agreement in 1864 to work the West Somerset Mineral Railway, from Watchet to the Brendon iron mines, for 55¼ years?

102   On 21 August 1895, during the Race to Scotland, an event occurred which prompted the North British signalman at Kinnaber Junction to allow the Caledonian train to proceed first. What was it?

103   How many of British Railways Standard class 5MT 4-6-0s were delivered fitted with Caprotti valve gear?

104   What was the 'Maid of Morven', introduced by the Caledonian Railway to the Callander and Oban line in 1914?

105   Who was the inventor of the oil-gas lighting system for carriages which originated in Prussia and first appeared in Britain on the Metropolitan Railway in 1876?

106   Which former Great Western Railway King class 4-6-0 was the first to be fitted with a double chimney in September 1955?

107   What was the original scheduled running time of the Great Western Railway's *Flying Dutchman* over the 193¾ miles from Paddington to Exeter?

108   Which standard gauge railway in Devon was physically unconnected to the rest of the British railway network?

109   Which of the former North Eastern Railway Raven A2 class Pacifics was rebuilt by Gresley with 'A1' type boiler and side-window cab in 1929?

110   What name was given to the small six-wheel vans containing generators for the electric lighting system that were marshalled in the Pullman trains of the London, Brighton & South Coast Railway from 1881?

111   What was the physical evidence of the improved steam collection arrangements in the boilers of the last batch of London & North Eastern Railway A3 Pacifics?

112   The National Railroad Passenger Corporation of the USA trades under the name 'Amtrak'. In which year was this organisation set up?

113   The Sand Hutton Light Railway in Yorkshire had four 1ft 6in gauge Hunslet 0-4-0Ts. Where had these locomotives been working before acquisition by the Sand Hutton Light Railway?

114   What is the name of the most northerly junction in Scotland?

115   Which was the last former Great Northern Railway Ivatt C1 class Atlantic to remain in British Railways service, withdrawn on 26 November 1950?

116   Where is the highest railway station in Europe and in what other respect is this station unusual, considering its situation?

117   Which major station reconstruction, including resignalling and the provision of quadruple track over 6¾ miles, was completed by the Great Western Railway in November 1935?

118   What was the furthest point west worked by Stockton & Darlington Railway locomotives?

119   What piece of railway-inspired music was used by the BBC as the signature tune for the radio detective serial *Paul Temple* in the 1950s?

120   What was the name of the London & North Western Railway's goods depot outside Fenchurch Street station in the City of London?

121   How did the London, Brighton & South Coast Railway Marsh J class 4-6-2Ts No 325 *Abergavenny* and No

326 *Bessborough* differ from each other?

122 In Paraguay what title was carried by the Ferrocarril Presidente Carlos Antonio Lopez, between Asunción and Encarnación, prior to nationalisation in 1961?

123 What was peculiar about the main line of the Northern Counties Committee main line between Belfast and Derry at Ballykelly, when the RAF operated from there?

124 Which is the only all steam country in the world?

125 Which Irish narrow gauge railway served the village of Blarney, giving access to Blarney Castle and the Blarney Stone?

126 In the film *The Titfield Thunderbolt*, which former Great Western Railway station appeared as 'Titfield'?

127 What was the name of the first six-coupled locomotive built by Timothy Hackworth at Shildon, in 1827?

128 In which town was there situated an engine shed named Edgeley?

129 What name was carried by Weston, Clevedon & Portishead Railway No 4, formerly Great Western Railway No 1384 and originally belonging to the Watlington & Princes Risborough Railway?

130 Which three Welsh railways made extensive use of somersault signals, as used on the Great Northern Railway and manufactured by Mackenzie & Holland, signal engineers?

131 What was the reply of William Vanderbilt when asked by a journalist whether his family ran the New York Central Railroad for the benefit of the public?

132 At the time of its greatest extent, what point of the British railway system was furthest, in terms of railway distance, from London?

133 Where on the Midland Railway was there a serious accident in 1910, the severity of which was exacerbated by the oil-gas lighting cylinders igniting?

134   Which Irish minor railway never numbered its locomotive stock, using only names for identification until closure in 1957?

135   Which was the first part of the Great Western Railway to be experimentally fitted with electrical cab signalling, later developed into the Great Western's Automatic Train Control system?

136   Around the turn of the century, the Belgian State Railways placed in service several types of locomotive closely following the designs and practice of which British locomotive engineer?

137   Where on the Somerset & Dorset were assisting engines attached for the northbound climb to Masbury Summit?

138   What was the nature of the accident commemorated in *The Ballad of John Axon?*

139   What modification was made in 1937 to two LNER Sandringham class 4-6-0s prior to their use on the *East Anglian* expresses between Liverpool Street and Norwich?

140   Which king of a European country expressly wished that his funeral train should be hauled by steam locomotives, his wish being carried out on 24 January 1972?

PRIZE QUESTIONS
Miscellany
(indicate the correct answer on the entry form on page 133)

Q1   In what year did Charles Beyer join Richard Peacock to establish the Manchester locomotive building firm of Beyer Peacock & Co?

A   1854.
B   1852.
C   1856.
D   1850.

Q2   What were the names of the two signalmen who took most of the blame for the Quintinshill disaster on 22 May 1915?

A   Watt and McMichael.
B   Tinsley and Meakin.
C   Hutchinson and Kirkpatrick.
D   Graham and Druitt.

Q3   Which former London Midland & Scottish Railway Royal Scot class 4-6-0 was driven by Jack Warner in the 1949 film *Train of Events*?

A   No 46116 *Irish Guardsman*.
B   No 46126 *Royal Army Service Corps*.
C   No 46136 *The Border Regiment*.
D   No 46146 *The Rifle Brigade*.

Q4   Which was the only British narrow gauge railway successfully to carry standard gauge wagons on transporters?

A   Lynton & Barnstaple Railway.
B   The Southwold Railway.
C   The Welshpool & Llanfair Light Railway.
D   The Leek & Manifold Light Railway.

Q5   What was the number of the restaurant car belonging to the Compagnie Internationale des Wagons-Lits in which the Armistice was signed in 1918 and the French surrendered in 1940?

A   2919.
B   2519.

C 2419.
D 2619.

Q6 At what point did the Whitechapel & Bow Railway make a junction with the London, Tilbury & Southend Railway?

A Gas Factory Junction.
B Bow Junction.
C Campbell Road Junction.
D Burdett Road Junction.

Q7 In what year did the Amalgamated Society of Railway Servants become the National Union of Railwaymen?

A 1907.
B 1909.
C 1911.
D 1913.

Q8 In which town was the office from which Col H. F. Stephens ran his ramshackle light railway empire?

A Shrewsbury.
B Portmadoc.
C Sevenoaks.
D Tonbridge.

Q9 Which firm built a British steam-turbine electric locomotive to the design of Sir Hugh Reid and W. Ramsey in 1910?

A North British Locomotive Co.
B Armstrong Whitworth & Co.
C Vulcan Foundry.
D Beyer Peacock & Co.

Q10 Which Welsh railway company's coat of arms incorporated a goat?

A Cambrian Railways.
B Brecon & Merthyr Railway.
C Rhymney Railway.
D Taff Vale Railway.

Q11 Which was the only British railway company to have a special room for shareholders' meetings?

A Midland Railway.
B Great Western Railway.

C   London & North Western Railway.
D   North Eastern Railway.

Q12   In 1876, where did the Midland Railway halt its expresses to and from the north to allow passengers half an hour for refreshment, before the introduction of dining cars?

A   Sheffield.
B   Normanton.
C   Cudworth.
D   Chesterfield.

Q13   Which national railway system had stations at both Paradis and Hell?

A   Danish State Railways.
B   Swedish State Railways.
C   Norwegian State Railways.
D   Finnish State Railways.

Q14   Which was the only railway in the British Isles to operate 4-8-0 tender locomotives?

A   Barry Railway.
B   Cork, Bandon & South Coast Railway.
C   Londonderry & Lough Swilly Railway.
D   Lancashire & Yorkshire Railway.

Q15   What was the commodity for which the Snailbeach District Railway, a 2ft 4in gauge line in Shropshire, was originally built to carry?

A   Agricultural produce.
B   Coal.
C   Iron ore.
D   Lead.

Q16   Which French composer wrote a 'Mouvement Symphonique' which was named after a type of French locomotive, *Pacific 231*?

A   Honegger.
B   Poulenc.
C   Milhaud.
D   Ibert.

Q17   Which railway company commissioned a film entitled *The Romance of a Railway* to commemorate an anniversary?

A   Southern Railway.
B   London & North Eastern Railway.
C   Great Western Railway.
D   London Midland & Scottish Railway.

Q18   On what date did the *Coronation Scot* service from Euston to Glasgow on the London Midland & Scottish Railway enter public service?

A   5 July 1937.
B   3 July 1937.
C   30 June 1937.
D   25 July 1937.

Q19   Which British railway was the first to introduce regular corridor trains from 1892?

A   Midland Railway.
B   London & North Western Railway.
C   Great Western Railway.
D   Great Northern Railway.

Q20   At which London terminus was John Schlesinger's film *Terminus* shot?

A   Charing Cross.
B   Waterloo.
C   Victoria.
D   London Bridge.

ANSWERS

ANSWERS
British Steam Locomotives

1   50psi.

2   Twenty-five.

3   Thomas Clarke Worsdell.

4   A large wooden barrel.

5   17½mph.

6   Braithwaite and Ericsson.

7   By means of a horse working on a treadmill.

8   *Perseverance*.

9   *Northumbrian*.

10   *Invicta*.

11   *Planet,* a 2-2-0.

12   2-2-2, with cylinders under the smokebox, sandwich frames and the trailing axle in the rear of the firebox.

13   The Brampton Railway, near Carlisle.

14   Todd, Kitson & Laird of Liverpool.

15   The 5ft 6in gauge New Orleans Railway in the southern USA.

16   *Vulcan,* one of the 2-2-2s built by Charles Tayleur & Co, Vulcan Foundry, Newton-le-Willows.

17   *Aeolus,* a Tayleur 2-2-2.

18   T. E. Harrison, the well-known civil engineer.

19   *Morning Star* had 6ft 6in diameter driving wheels, the others had 7ft drivers.

20   The Allan 2-2-2 No 49 *Columbine,* now preserved in the National Railway Museum, York.

21   The Gooch 2-2-2 *Great Western*.

22   Francis Trevithick.

23   Bury, Curtis & Kennedy.

24   Stothert, Slaughter & Co.

25 *Lord of the Isles.*

26 Great Northern Railway No 215, built in 1853 and scrapped in 1870.

27 *Lion* was sold to the Mersey Docks and Harbour Board as a stationary boiler.

28 943 (857 for the London & North Western Railway and an additional 86 for the Lancashire & Yorkshire Railway).

29 The Stockton & Darlington Railway.

30 The Furness Railway. (One of these late Bury engines, 'Coppernob', may be seen at the National Railway Museum, York.)

31 Fifty-three, all built at Doncaster.

32 Nos 224 and 264, built for the North British Railway in 1871 to the design of T. Wheatley.

33 No 71 *Wapping*, closely followed by No 72 *Fenchurch* and No 70 *Poplar*.

34 The Skye Bogies for the line from Dingwall to Strome Ferry, later extended to Kyle of Lochalsh.

35 East & West Junction Railway No 1 (an 0-6-6-0 Fairlie type locomotive built in 1876). This is a very obscure and poorly documented engine. The single Fairlie 0-4-4T on the Swindon & Marlborough Railway was the first to do any useful work.

36 Unlike the neighbouring Metropolitan Railway, where the original engines bore names, the Metropolitan District Railway engines were lettered A to Z, with no 'I' or 'O', thus identifying the twenty-four engines.

37 The Mersey Railway, between Liverpool and Birkenhead via steeply graded tunnels under the River Mersey.

38 The Edinburgh International Exhibition of 1886.

39 'Cauliflowers'. (The armorial device of the LNWR, displayed on the engine's centre splasher, resembled a cauliflower when seen from a distance.)

40 The inside valve was operated by means of a single-slip eccentric, which meant that the low-pressure valve events were not under the control of the driver

41   The Worsdell-von Borries two-cylinder system.

42   The Swedish & Norwegian Railway, from the Swedish iron mines to the Norwegian port of Narvik.

43   No 240 *Onward*.

44   230. (There were 280 'Ironclads', but the final 50 remained as tender engines.)

45   Manchester, Sheffield & Lincolnshire Railway 9C class 0-6-2T No 7, built at Gorton, Manchester, in 1891. This engine was later London & North Eastern Railway No 5515 and was withdrawn in 1956 as British Railways No 69250.

46   Dean 3021 class 2-2-2 No 3028, completed in August 1891 as a 'convertible' with broad gauge wheels outside both sets of frames; it was converted to standard gauge in August 1892.

47   *Bulkeley*, an Iron Duke class 4-2-2 built at Swindon in 1880.

48   *Stag* and *Leopard*.

49   No 760 *Petrolea*.

50   The Highland Railway.

51   7ft 7¼in. (These were the largest coupled wheels ever used in the United Kingdom.)

52   The Glasgow & South Western Railway. The engine was later rebuilt with a larger boiler and carried the name *Lord Glenarthur*.

53   No 720, a T7 class; it was a four-cylinder simple expansion engine with uncoupled driving wheels, like a London & North Western Railway Webb compound.

54   No 1304 *Jeanie Deans*.

55   Ten locomotives of Great Northern Railway class A4, designed by H. A Ivatt, and built at Doncaster in 1901.

56   The acceleration of a 300 ton passenger train from rest to a speed of 30mph in 30 seconds.

57   No 3297 *Earl Cawdor*.

58   Churchward City class 4-4-0 No 3440 *City of Truro*.

59   Vulcan Foundry, Newton-le-Willows.

60   The engine was rebuilt as an 0-8-0, retaining the same

number, which was used for goods traffic until scrapped in 1913.

61 The engines were rebuilt as 2-6-2Ts with taper boilers, intended for Birmingham suburban traffic.

62 'Humpty Dumpties'. (This nickname applied only to those reboilered engines which retained the 2-4-0 wheel arrangement.)

63 The John Hick class 2-2-2-2s, the last of which were withdrawn in 1912.

64 The D15 class 4-4-0s, built at Eastleigh in 1912.

65 Stumpf 'Uniflow' cylinders, in which steam admission is controlled by valves in the usual way, but exhaust is controlled by the piston itself, uncovering the exhaust port situated in the centre of the cylinder bore.

66 Borsig of Berlin.

67 *Knight of the Black Eagle* (removed on account of the German associations of the name).

68 The 'Austrian' goods class.

69 Billinton E5 class 0-6-2T No 591 *Tillington*.

70 Midland Railway No 2290, built at Derby in 1919 ('Big Bertha', the Lickey banker, latterly British Railways No 58100).

71 The 2-8-0 goods engine No 461 (GNR and LNER class 02).

72 Woolwich Arsenal.

73 No 333 *Remembrance*.

74 The engine had been sold to the Wirral Railway in 1921 and was renumbered with the rest of the Wirral stock in 1923 instead of reverting to its original identity. The error was never rectified and the engine was withdrawn in 1952 as No 46762.

75 No 2925 *Saint Martin*, renumbered 4900, and retaining the same name.

76 North Staffordshire Railway 0-6-0T No 23, built at Stoke to the design of John A. Hookham in 1922 and converted in 1924 to an 0-6-0 tender engine. It was withdrawn in 1928 as London Midland & Scottish Railway No 2367.

77 The S. W. Johnson 4-4-0 No 1757, named *Beatrice*,

and the Johnson 'Spinner' 4-2-2 No 2601, named *Princess of Wales*.

78 The twenty-four modified Directors (class D11/2) were sent to Scotland to work the former North British Railway lines, where there was a shortage of suitable engines for passenger traffic.

79 The five London & North Western Railway Prince of Wales class 4-6-0s with inside cylinders but outside Walschaert's valve gear, working the valves by means of rocking levers.

80 *Viscount Churchill*.

81 LNER No 4419, formerly GNR No 1419, built at Doncaster in 1906.

82 No 4009 *Shooting Star*, renumbered and renamed as 100 A1 *Lloyds* in 1936.

83 For use as a banking engine helping loaded coal trains up the 1 in 40 Worsborough Incline near Barnsley.

84 No 4079 *Pendennis Castle*.

85 No 859 *Lord Hood*.

86 Class A1 Pacific No 2562 *Isinglass* and class P1 2-8-2 No 2394.

87 No 1974 *Howe* of the Alfred the Great class, never renumbered by the LMS and withdrawn as No 1974 in 1928.

88 Peter Drummond's superheated 137 class, built for the Glasgow & South Western Railway, with a weight for the engine alone of 61 tons 17cwts.

89 Ten.

90 Three (Nos 4997-9, the other thirty of the class were fitted with steam brakes only).

91 Class Z.

92 6399 *Fury*.

93 450psi.

94 As 4-6-0 tender engines (Southern Railway class N15X, lasting in BR service until the late 1950s).

95 6152 *The King's Dragoon Guardsman*.

96 LMS No 25001 *Snowdon* (originally LNWR No

2191), withdrawn in 1934.

97   King class 4-6-0 No 6014 *King Henry VII* and Castle class 4-6-0 No 5005 *Manorbier Castle*.

98   LMS No 14010, formerly Caledonian Railway No 123, used between Perth and Dundee until 1935.

99   112½mph.

100   No 3265 *Tre Pol and Pen*.

101   Great Western Railway Barnum or 3206 class 2-4-0 No 3222, withdrawn in March 1937.

102   No 2751 *Humorist*.

103   C1 (the 'C', as third letter of the alphabet, indicated an engine with three driving axles).

104   The lightweight 2-6-2 design class V4. These engines appeared after the death of Sir Nigel, only two were built and the design was not perpetuated by Sir Nigel's successor, Edward Thompson.

105   No 365 *The Morpeth*.

106   410.

107   Two (LMS Nos 7456 and 7553, NCC Nos 18 and 19).

108   *The Queen's Edinburgh*.

109   7337 (later 77337. This engine never became British Railways' property and remained in the hands of the army until scrapped at Longmoor in 1965).

110   The East Kent Railway, which had acquired the engine from the Ridham surplus depot; the Government had bought the engine from the LSWR to shunt there in 1917.

111   Nicholson Thermic Syphons.

112   The 48XX number series was required for the renumbering of the 28XX 2-8-0s which were scheduled for conversion to oil burning.

113   No 2546, later British Railways No 62546, scrapped in June 1957.

114   No 6022 *King Edward III*.

115   No 68 (LNER numbering) *Sir Visto*.

116   No 119.

117 British Railways No 46243 *City of Lancaster*, de-streamlined in 1949.

118 No 45522 *Prestatyn*.

119 These engines were given boilers fitted with steel fireboxes, rather than the usual copper firebox.

120 The engine fell down the hoist shaft leading to the Waterloo & City tube at Waterloo and had to be recovered piecemeal.

121 Two (No 36001 actually steamed, No 36002 was nearly complete and No 36003 was in an advanced stage of construction).

122 British Railways No 32039 *Hartland Point*, originally London, Brighton & South Coast Railway No 39, built at Brighton in 1905.

123 The two engines, Nos 44686-7, were built at Horwich, Lancashire.

124 No 46205 had her inside valves operated by rocking levers from the outside valve gear, the rest of the class having four independent sets of valve gear.

125 Crewe works.

126 *Amethyst* (after the HMS *Amethyst* which achieved fame in the Yangtze incident of 1949).

127 The engine was named at a ceremony on 30 January 1951 at Marylebone station.

128 At the Festival of Britain on the South Bank in London.

129 Nos 70043-4. (At the time of delivery these engines were unnamed; they were later named *Earl Kitchener* and *Earl Haig* respectively.)

130 No 71000 was authorised as a replacement for the rebuilt Stainer Pacific No 46202 *Princess Anne*, which was originally turbine driven before rebuilding and which was damaged beyond repair in the Harrow disaster on 5 October 1952.

131 70047.

132 No 46137 *The Prince of Wales's Volunteers (South Lancashire)*, converted at Crewe in March 1955.

133 No 35018 *British India Line*, rebuilt at Eastleigh.

134   Former London, Brighton & South Coast No 357, once named *Riddlesdown*, survived on the Whittingham Mental Asylum Railway, a private branch line near Preston, Lancashire, until 1957.

135   Ten (Nos 92020-9). The engines were altered to normal draughting, with the Crosti arrangement blanked off, late in their lives.

136   Berkley Mechanical Stokers.

137   The N7 class, of which the great majority were allocated to Stratford depot and used for suburban work in north-east London.

138   The engine was fitted with a Giesl Oblong Ejector Chimney, an Austrian device intended to improve steaming on inferior coal.

139   No 60052 *Prince Palatine*.

140   It was proposed to build a further fifteen Clan class Pacifics, ten for the Scottish Region, to carry further 'Clan' names, and five for the Southern Region, to be named after Anglo-Saxon worthies.

141   Stanier's ten 2P 0-4-4T introduced in 1932.

142   *Valour*.

143   London & South Western Railway class T14 4-6-0.

144   London, Brighton & South Coast Railway 0-6-0T Terriers (No 646 *Newington* and No 668 *Clapham*).

145   North British Railway, built at Cowlairs in 1868 by Wheatley.

ANSWERS
British Railway History

1   Huntingdon Beaumont, a landed proprietor and colliery owner.

2   In connection with the Pensnett Railway near Stourbridge, Staffordshire, in 1681.

3   A wooden colliery wagonway between Tranent and Cockenzie, about 10 miles east of Edinburgh.

4   1725.

5   Ralph Allan (1694–1764).

6   The Middleton Railway near Leeds, built under an Act granted to Charles Brandling on 9 June 1758.

7   27 September 1825.

8   25 July 1834.

9   The Bill for the London & Southampton Railway was passed by Parliament without the gauge clause, presumably as an oversight; the Great Western board was quick to exploit the precedent.

10   31 August 1835.

11   Thomas Edmondson.

12   Between Paddington (old station) and Maidenhead Riverside (later Taplow).

13   Fixed engines and cable traction.

14   By sea from Fleetwood to Ardrossan.

15   30 June 1841.

16   30 June 1840.

17   Bishopsgate.

18   The Great North of England Railway.

19   14 June 1841.

20   Taunton.

21   The Bodmin & Wadebridge Railway.

22   Between Louth and New Holland, Lincolnshire.

23   10½ hours.

24   2 February 1874.

25   The Great Western and Midland railways.

26   9 January 1886.

27   1898.

28   1915.

29   30 April 1972.

30   1838.

31   1800.

32   The Merstham Greystone lime works, 18 miles by railway from Wandsworth Wharf.

33   25 March 1807.

34   Edward Pease.

35   Thomas Meynell of Yarm.

36   Moreton-in-Marsh.

37   6 May 1833.

38   The Denbigh Hall Inn and Rugby station.

39   Gloucester, where the Great Western Railway met the Birmingham & Gloucester Railway.

40   1844.

41   The St Helens & Runcorn Gap Railway and the Sankey Brook Navigation Canal Co.

42   Dr John Keate.

43   1 December 1847.

44   The London & Croydon Railway.

45   1 August 1848. Through traffic to Holyhead did not commence until 1850, pending completion of the Britannia Bridge across the Menai Strait.

46   Hitchin and King's Cross.

47   The Cornwall Railway (Plymouth-Truro).

48   1862.

49   1862.

50   The Great Northern Railway.

51 The Sirhowy Railway between Nine Mile Point and Nantybwch.

52 1 November 1875.

53 1 January 1876.

54 1 May 1876.

55 21 January 1876.

56 The Imperial Tramways Co, Bristol.

57 The Great Northern Railway, on the principal expresses between King's Cross and Leeds.

58 David Davies, of the Ocean Coal Co.

59 The 3rd Duke of Sutherland, who had built the line out of his own pocket and sold it to the Highland in 1884.

60 James Staats Forbes.

61 Huntingdon East.

62 1899.

63 The Manchester, Sheffield & Lincolnshire Railway, later the Great Central, the Midland Railway and the Great Northern Railway.

64 Cornelius Lundie.

65 J. A. (later Sir John) Aspinall.

66 Aylesbury station was jointly owned by two concerns that were themselves joint committees (Great Western & Great Central Joint and the Metropolitan and Great Central Joint committees).

67 Sam Fay (later Sir Sam and general manager of the Great Central Railway).

68 The Great Western Railway operated a motor bus service from Helston to The Lizard from 17 August 1903.

69 Great Western Railway and the Rhymney Railway.

70 Sir Frederick Harrison.

71 The Lancashire & Yorkshire and the North Eastern railways.

72 1 January 1908.

73 24 April 1924.

74 2 June 1924.

75   The Hundred of Manhood & Selsey Tramway.

76   A fire at the depot at St Aubin destroyed most of the rolling stock.

77   1 October 1936.

78   1953.

79   Great Moor Street.

80   January 1955.

81   The Midland Railway.

82   The Glasgow, Paisley, Kilmarnock & Ayr and the Glasgow, Dumfries & Carlisle railways.

83   1858.

84   *The Brighton Pullman Limited.*

85   Cannon Street.

86   The Lancashire & Yorkshire Railway with twenty-three at the grouping, plus four jointly owned with the London & North Western.

87   Between Pontrilas on the Newport, Abergavenny & Hereford section of the Great Western Railway, and a junction with the Midland Railway at Hay-on-Wye.

88   1893.

89   1866.

90   The Manchester, Sheffield & Lincolnshire Railway.

91   The Great Central, Great Northern and Great Eastern railways.

92   The London, Chatham & Dover Railway.

93   The Glasgow & South Western and Caledonian railways, for alternate periods of three years each.

94   The Great Northern Railway.

95   The Highland Railway, using an engine and rolling stock specially transferred.

96   Liverpool (Riverside) to connect with transatlantic liners, at that time sailing from Liverpool.

97   The South Wales Railway and the West Midland Railway.

98   Sir Daniel Gooch, Brunel's original locomotive superintendent.

99   The Leicester & Swannington Railway.

100   The Swansea Vale Railway.

101   The Newcastle & Carlisle Railway.

102   25 June 1877.

103   Newcastle and Berwick.

104   Bishopsgate.

105   1844.

106   Sir Richard Moon.

107   1903.

108   1 September 1968.

109   1849.

110   1866.

111   Coal for the Home Fleet, at that time based at Scapa Flow.

112   30 September 1972.

113   Rhydyfelin, 8¾ miles from Heath Junction, Cardiff.

114   1859.

115   Pending completion of Brunel's suspension bridge over the River Wye at Chepstow.

116   1861.

117   First Lord of the Admiralty.

118   London Road, reached by running powers over the Manchester, Sheffield & Lincolnshire Railway from New Mills Junction.

119   1872.

120   Thomas Cook.

121   John Ellis, a former director of the Leicester & Swannington Railway.

122   1870.

123   Retford.

124   1862.

125   The original terminus was at Lees Street, off Oldham Road.

126 The Wrexham, Mold & Connah's Quay Railway.

127 Lord Farringdon.

128 Between Quainton Road station and Canfield Place, St John's Wood, where the Great Central line diverged to Marylebone.

129 1859.

130 1908.

ANSWERS
British Railway Engineering

1　Ralph Wood.

2　105ft.

3　Chat Moss.

4　Joseph Locke.

5　Lord Wharncliffe, chairman of the Lords Committee on the GWR's Act of Incorporation.

6　36 million.

7　Philip Hardwick.

8　North of Tring.

9　Paddington and West Drayton (extended to Slough in 1843).

10　5ft.

11　William Cubitt.

12　The Royal Border Bridge, Berwick-upon-Tweed.

13　The Imperial Riding School, Moscow.

14　Nine (Gas Works, Copenhagen, Wood Green, Barnet, Hadley South, Hadley North, Potters Bar, Welwyn South, Welwyn North).

15　The Royal Albert Bridge over the River Tamar at Saltash.

16　Melton Constable, Norfolk.

17　Langley, south of Stevenage.

18　Sevenoaks (1 mile, 1,693yd).

19　Wembley Park, Middlesex.

20　Walnut Tree.

21　The Somerset & Dorset Joint Railway.

22　The Taff Vale Railway, between Cardiff and Merthyr Tydfil.

23　Machen.

24   Henry Robinson, engineer of the Shrewsbury & Chester Railway.

25   Mochdre on the Chester–Holyhead section.

26   James Manson.

27   £500.

28   Stationary engines and cable haulage.

29   17 September 1838.

30   22 January 1822.

31   Just over 1 mile, from South Street, Canterbury, to Bogshole Farm.

32   1,484ft.

33   Part of the Chequerbent incline on the former London & North Western Railway line from Leigh to Bolton acquired a gradient of 1 in 19½ for a short distance following mining subsidence.

34   On the London & Birmingham Railway between Euston and Camden in 1837.

35   2 miles, 241yd.

36   Reinforced concrete.

37   On a specially built track straddling the London & North Eastern Railway line near Milngavie, Dunbartonshire.

38   £99,000.

39   113ft.

40   This displayed an illuminated fishtail shape alongside the lamp on distant signals, making distant signals more easily distinguishable at night, before the adoption of yellow glass in distant-signal spectacles from 1925.

41   Charing Cross, South Eastern & Chatham Railway.

42   Round Down Cliff, a small promontory. Removal by dynamite was considered cheaper than tunnelling through it.

43   2,684yd.

44   1 October 1885.

45   Beaumont's Egg (from the French *beau montage*).

46   The City of Leicester's Swithland Reservoir.

47 On the water balance system, a loaded water tank descending the incline to draw wagons up, the empty tank returning to the top drawn by the weight of descending wagons.

48 24 November 1859.

49 1830.

50 310 acres.

51 Firebrick.

52 1904.

53 Inverurie.

54 Standedge Tunnel, between Diggle and Marsden.

55 The branch from St Erth to St Ives in Cornwall, opened on 1 June 1877.

56 The former South Wales Railway from Gloucester (Grange Court Junction) to Swansea.

57 Alaric Hope.

58 The Gloucester & Berkeley Canal. (All the spans over the River Severn were fixed.)

59 The Ouse.

60 Carn Brea, near Penzance.

61 At Crewe North engine shed on the London & North Western Railway.

62 1 mile, 340yd.

63 William Henry Barlow.

64 George Parker Bidder.

65 Sir John Wolfe-Barry.

66 Alexander McDonnell.

67 The London & North Western Railway rolled its own rails at Crewe.

68 Nineteen.

69 Romford Factory (later used by the Stores Dept).

70 Joseph Mitchell.

71 James Brunlees and Douglas Fox.

72 1839.

73   John Foster.

74   1,060 tons.

75   On a level stretch of the Midland Railway near Newark-on-Trent.

76   Torpantau Tunnel on the Brecon & Merthyr Railway, with a west portal at 1,313ft above sea level.

77   C. A. Park.

78   Chelfham Viaduct (eight spans, 70ft high).

79   Nine Elms, London.

80   1844.

ANSWERS
Foreign Railways

1   Paris–Menton, on the Riviera.

2   4 December 1876.

3   1 October 1920.

4   Peter Cooper.

5   1909.

6   Furka Base Tunnel, exceeding the Gotthard Tunnel. (The Simplon Tunnel is longer but is partly in Italy.) 15.407km.

7   5 years, 3 months and 23 days, the line opening on 26 September 1855.

8   Helsinki and the garrison town of Hämeenlinna, 65 miles away.

9   Northern Railway of France No 701, a 2-2-2-0 with uncoupled driving wheels like a Webb compound, built by the Société Alsacienne des Constructions Mechaniques at Mulhouse.

10   Danish State Railways P class, still extant in 1966.

11   Owencarrow Viaduct, County Donegal.

12   Marc Seguin (1786–1875).

13   The Camden & Amboy Railroad.

14   John Cockerill of Seraing.

15   Der Ludwigsbahn (Nuremburg-Fürth).

16   2 metres.

17   1854.

18   Lord Strathcona (Donald Smith).

19   Deutsche Bundesbahn No 038-313-3, operating from Tübingen.

20   5 June 1883.

21   Haydarpasa.

22   1901.

23   Athens to Piraeus (6¼ miles).

24   Abbas I.

25   The Rama VI Bridge.

26   On the Canadian Pacific Railway main line through the Rockies between Banff and Field on the western descent of the mountains through Kicking Horse Pass. They lie five miles west of the Continental Divide.

27   Introduced in 1957, it is a connecting network of luxury daytime first-class only international expresses linking much of Europe. Most have since been replaced by first- and second-class luxury inter-city services.

28   Between the middle and upper levels on the internal railway system of the Guinness brewery in Dublin.

29   Union Pacific No 119 and the Central Pacific's *Jupiter*.

30   Zimbabwe and Zambia. Cleveland Bridge & Engineering Co, Darlington.

31   Altoona, Pennsylvania.

32   4-8-4.

33   0-8-0 switcher No 244, built by the Norfolk & Western Railroad at Roanoke, Virginia.

34   The Hindenburgdamm.

35   1 metre.

36   The E10 class 4-8-0s, introduced in 1946, ten being built in 1946 by Nohab.

37   Two 0-6-6-0 Kitson Meyer tank engines built by Kitson in 1903 (works Nos 4240 and 4241), shipped out in parts and re-erected at Umtali workshops on Rhodesia Railways.

38   Richmond, Virginia.

39   12 January 1929.

40   The Monson Railroad.

41   2 September 1935.

42   Great Southern Railway, and later the Great Southern Railways.

43   The bridge was designed to be dismantled every

autumn and re-erected every spring, as it stood in the path of regular avalanches.

44   Jawn Henry.

45   Atbara.

46   Nairobi.

47   National Railways of Peru (formerly Southern Railway of Peru).

48   Lima, Alco and Baldwin.

49   1,340.

50   Lethbridge Viaduct.

51   *Bhowani Junction*.

52   The Northern Railway of France.

53   Gotthard.

54   Zeppelins.

55   Algeria.

56   Durango-Silverton; Antonito-Chama.

57   The line connected the Prussian State Railways at Wesel with the Dutch State Railway at Boxtel.

58   5 April 1855.

59   The Chicago, Milwaukee, St Paul & Pacific Railroad. The locomotives were used on the high-speed *Hiawatha* service between Chicago and Minneapolis.

60   1.524 metres or 5ft.

61   Patiala. (Two lines were operated under the direction of Col C. W. Bowles, between Patiala City and Sunam, and Sirhind and Morinda.)

62   1 October 1968.

63   *La Portena*.

64   The 75cm gauge line from Samsun on the Black Sea coast to Carsamba.

65   The Dundalk, Newry & Greenore Railway.

66   The line from Porte Vincennes to Porte Maillot.

67   5ft.

68   1878.

69 Ecuador.

70 The Highland Railway Castle class.

71 3 metres.

72 11 January 1969, locomotive No 231 K 82.

73 1963.

74 The Dutch Rhenish Railway.

75 No 2850 was used to haul the royal train carrying King George VI and Queen Elizabeth across Canada in May 1939, and the king gave his permission for the name to be given to the whole class. Every engine had a crown applied to the valencing.

76 C. E. Spagnoletti.

77 The working of the heavy German mail trains between Boxtel and Flushing.

78 Pakistan.

79 J. B. Flamme.

80 1923.

81 The Graz-Koflacher Bahn.

82 Those railroads whose operating revenue exceeds 5 million dollars per annum.

83 Connaught Tunnel, opened 6 December 1916.

84 The 5ft gauge Panama Railroad, 48 miles long, connecting Aspinwall (Colon) with Panama.

85 29 November 1969.

86 The Patapsco River.

87 The 2ft 6in gauge railway operated by Ramal Ferro Industries Rio Turbio in southern Argentina connecting the Rio Turbio coal mines with the coast at Rio Gallegos, 162 miles away.

88 24 August 1867.

89 297 miles.

90 The Chinese Eastern Railway, built by the Russians on Manchurian territory.

91 Henry Meiggs (1811–77).

92 The 800mm gauge Mount Pilatus Railway in Switzer-

land with a gradient of 1 in 2, using the Locher type of rack with horizontal teeth.

93   44.

94   Roanoke, Virginia.

95   1924 (Railway Act of 30 August 1924, subsequently amended by the Railway Act of 13 March 1930).

96   The 200km between Paris (Quai d'Orsay) and Vierzon.

97   Isambard Kingdom Brunel.

98   Albury. (The break of gauge remained here until 1962.)

99   The *Orange Express* from Cape Town to Durban.

100   Ferrocarril General Roca.

101   Huey Pierce Long, the spectacularly corrupt, crypto-fascist governor of Louisiana in the 1920s.

102   Bay Area Rapid Transit.

103   The Rimutaka Incline.

104   *The Broadway Limited*.

105   (Robert Francis) Fairlie.

106   New York and New Orleans.

107   The threat by British Columbia to secede from the Empire if communications with the rest of Canada were not improved.

108   The Mount Cenis pass.

109   1931. (The stock still exists and is occasionally used by MOB and RhB.)

110   The Canadian Pacific Railway.

111   *The Anatolia Express*.

112   The small station known as Berlin Zoo (Zoologisches Garten).

113   The Hohenzollern Bridge.

114   The Egyptian State Railways, for use on the Cairo-Luxor expresses.

115   The death of the designer, Gaston du Bousquet.

116   The Prussian-controlled Alsace-Lorraine Railways.

117   Mitropa.

118   The Hoosac Tunnel.

119   Gustave Eiffel.

120   1925.

121   Henry Morrison Flagler, a founder of the Standard Oil Co.

122   Russia.

123   1,775 miles.

124   103.

125   7,407ft.

126   The Salzkammergutlokalbahn.

127   The line was destroyed in the 1944 eruption of Mount Vesuvius.

128   The Retiro terminus in Buenos Aires, Argentina.

129   Kharagpur in Bihar state, on the former Bengal & Nagpur Railway, with a length of 2,733ft.

130   1892.

131   Because the rolling stock and engines were second-hand from India where the metre gauge was well established.

132   Imperial Ottoman Hedjaz Railway. 3ft 5½in.

ANSWERS
Diesel and Electric Locomotives and Railways

1   Brush type 4 No D1733.

2   *Kestrel* was sold to the railway administration of the USSR.

3   Bristol (Bath Road).

4   The Deutsche Bundesbahn V200 class.

5   North British Locomotive Co, Springburn, Glasgow.

6   The Western Region diesel-hydraulic D600 *Active* which went into traffic on 24 January 1958, predating the English Electric type 4 (BR class 40) by three months.

7   D1035 *Western Yeoman*.

8   10100.

9   650hp.

10   512 (D1500–1999 and D1100–11).

11   The British Railways Standard class 5MT 4–6–0.

12   D0260 *Lion*.

13   E1000, a rebuild of the former Western Region gas-turbine locomotive No 18100, used for crew training and equipment testing between Mauldeth Road and Wilmslow on the Manchester–Crewe line.

14   Doncaster.

15   The Pakistan Western Railway took delivery of twenty-nine locomotives supplied by the British Rail Traction group and built by Metro-Cammell.

16   No 87 101, later named *Stephenson*.

17   Cuban National Railways.

18   The 8.35am Euston–Liverpool on Monday 25 November 1965, hauled by class AL6 No E3171.

19   205.6mph.

20   5 January 1970.

21   No E3009.

22   The Giant's Causeway Tramway in Ireland, electrified in 1883.

23   Liverpool Street to Chelmsford, completed 11 June 1956, and Shenfield to Southend (Victoria), completed 31 December 1956. Both sections were converted to 25kV ac in 1960.

24   This was a narrow gauge line 600yd long, working at 150V dc from a central rail and installed in the grounds of the Berlin Trades Exhibition in 1879.

25   August 1972.

26   The 4–COR units built for the Portsmouth electrification in 1937.

27   Unit No 3052.

28   1893.

29   Swiss Federal Railways Re 6/6 7,800kW (1 hour rating) 10,455hp.

30   D9000/55 001 *Royal Scots Grey*.

31   Gas turbine electric; Brown Boveri (Switzerland).

32   Birmingham Railway Carriage & Wagon Co, Sulzer, Associated Electrical Industries.

33   1894; 4 wheel locomotive with a Priestman vertical twin-cylinder engine of 12hp, demonstrated for shunting on the Hull & Barnsley at Alexandra Docks.

34   Great Britain with the prototype HST at 141mph (227kph) between York and Northallerton on 11 July 1973.

35   Ford Motor Co, Dagenham. One is preserved on the Kent & East Sussex Railway.

36   The Post Office Railway.

37   London & North Western Railway; Willesden–Earls Court; Siemens.

38   France with a specially geared TGV which reached 236.12mph (380kph) on 26 February 1981.

39   Tyne & Wear Metro.

40   Great Britain with the experimental APT-E which reached 151mph (243kph) between Reading and Didcot on 3 August 1975.

ANSWERS
Miscellany

ERRATUM
Please note that the following answers should be transposed:
33 & 36   72 & 82   83 & 87

1 The former Great Western Railway King class 4–6–0 No 6000 *King George V*.

2 Household refuse for dumping at tips on the Dunstable and Hertford branches.

3 King's Cross, Peterborough, Bradford and Leeds.

4 The locomotives and stock ran with the wheel flanges *outside* the rails.

5 Former M&GN No 55, built by Dübs of Glasgow in 1900; later LNER J3 class 0–6–0 No 085, rebuilt to class J4 in 1937, renumbered 4160 in 1946 and withdrawn as British Railways No 64160 in 1951.

6 *The Great Train Robbery*.

7 John Ford.

8 *General*, built by Cooke & Co for the Western & Atlantic Railroad in 1855.

9 *Rome Express*.

10 The Reading–Basingstoke branch.

11 Cliddesden.

12 The Merthyr, Tredegar & Abergavenny Railway.

13 No 1462.

14 Emile Zola.

15 West side pilot at Liverpool Street station.

16 Hunslet Engine Co, Leeds.

17 To provide spectacular footage for an air raid sequence for John Frankenheimer's film *The Train*.

18 66.3mph.

19 Eight: *Wren* (now preserved), *Robin*, *Dot*, *Fly*, *Wasp*, *Midget*, *Mouse* and *Bee*.

20 Kent & East Sussex Railway.

21 On the Midland section between Derby and St Pancras.

22   Three: Shepherd's Bush, Hammersmith & City line; Shepherd's Bush, Central London Railway; Shepherd's Bush, London & South Western Railway Addison Road–Richmond line. These three co-existed between 1900–16.

23   The railway was immediately closed, the track ripped up and the rails, engines and rolling stock shipped to Formosa where they were dumped on a beach and left to rot.

24   *Hatter's Castle.*

25   Dr Crova.

26   The Midland & South Western Junction Railway took delivery of a 2–6–0, No 14, which had been left on Beyer Peacock's hands by the failure of a South American company, and later ordered a second similar engine, No 16.

27   Allan straight link valve gear.

28   Brick red.

29   1871.

30   London Transport services north of Rickmansworth.

31   Ivatt class 2MT 2–6–2T No 41272, built in 1950.

32   They were converted to observation cars to run on the Southern Railway's *Devon Belle* all-Pullman train.

33   The 4ft 6in gauge horse-worked Lee Moor Tramway.

34   Chicago.

35   The London, Chatham & Dover Railway. (The GNR and LCDR ran a joint service from Hatfield to Herne Hill via the Metropolitan widened lines.)

36   Ashton-under-Lyne.

37   The Van Railway.

38   Uruguay.

39   By sea from Newcastle to London and thence by canal barge to the company's wharf at West Drayton.

40   Lord Beeching.

41   *Dunrobin.*

42   'Invisible green' — in fact, black showing a tinge of green in certain lighting conditions.

43   *Jupiter*, formerly on the Midland Railway and run on the London, Chatham & Dover Railway between 1882–4.

44 The engine was covered in red and cream wallpaper in the course of making a commercial for a well-known brand of wallpaper paste.

45 For working on the Pwllyrhebog Incline near Treherbert, a rope-assisted incline with a maximum gradient of 1 in 13, up to Clydach Vale Colliery.

46 Madame Adelina Patti, who lived at Craig-y-Nos Castle.

47 Claude Monet.

48 The Stephenson Locomotive Society *Jubilee Requiem* special from King's Cross to Newcastle and return on 24 October 1964 with No 60009 *Union of South Africa*.

49 After the fall of France it became impossible to obtain the paper rolls used in these French-made machines.

50 Georgius Agricola (Georg Bauer) 1494–1555.

51 About 5ft 4in (within remarkably close limits).

52 DX class 0–6–0.

53 The exhaust-steam injector, using exhaust steam to work boiler water feed apparatus.

54 As a counter-pressure engine for testing.

55 The London & South Western Railway Servants Orphanage, later the Southern Railwaymen's Home for Children.

56 The small-boilered 2–6–0s (GNR class H2, LNER class K1).

57 1926.

58 Lots Road, Chelsea.

59 The RODs were fitted with steam brakes only and therefore could not use the standard GWR ATC which required vacuum power for its operation.

60 The Furness Railway (Nos 12A and 35, Sharp Stewart works Nos 1017 and 1707).

61 In the Nederlandse Spoorwegen headquarters at Utrecht, Holland.

62 Nos 70035–39.

63 No 2508 *Brown Jack*.

64 Rugby.

65   Four: Dowlais Top, Brecon & Merthyr Railway; Dowlais Central, Brecon & Merthyr Railway; Dowlais High Street, London & North Western Railway; Dowlais Cae Harris, Taff Bargoed Joint.

66   No 4466 *Herring Gull*.

67   Armagh.

68   Caledonian Railway Dunalastair IV class 4–4–0 No 139, delivered in 1910.

69   Neasden.

70   Twenty-two.

71   Class D three-cylinder compound 0–8–0.

72   The southern terminus at Dingle.

73   On the Liverpool & Manchester Railway on 11 November 1830.

74   East St Louis, Illinois, on the Mississippi River, opposite St Louis, Missouri.

75   Material for motorway construction.

76   Four (known at Dunalastair I to IV).

77   Midland Railway Kirtley 0–6–0.

78   North Road works, Darlington.

79   Much of the day's service was cancelled to allow the running of Queen Victoria's funeral train from Paddington to Windsor, together with special trains carrying mourners.

80   Cumbres & Toltec Scenic Railroad, Colorado/New Mexico, USA.

81   Solway Viaduct.

82   Isle of Wight Central Railway.

83   Sodium acetate.

84   No 955 *Charles Dickens*.

85   London, Brighton & South Coast Railway Gladstone class 0–4–2.

86   1928.

87   Sunderland.

88   No 1309 *Adriatic*.

89 *Leviathan*.

90 Edinburgh Waverley as expanded in 1892.

91 Norton Fitzwarren, west of Taunton.

92 The NBR 165 class 0–6–0T (LNER class J82).

93 Fifty-six.

94 William Powell Frith (1819–1909).

95 Swindon.

96 *The Railway Children*.

97 1956 (BR No 7711, withdrawn in 1961 as LT No L90).

98 Giesl oblong ejector chimney.

99 Dark red with gilt lettering.

100 Former London, Brighton & South Coast Railway H2 class No 32424 *Beachy Head*, withdrawn in 1958.

101 The Ebbw Vale Steel, Iron and Coal Co.

102 Both trains arrived together and the North British signalman acted in a sporting manner by allowing the Caledonian train to take the road to Aberdeen.

103 Thirty (Nos 73125–54).

104 A Pullman observation car.

105 Julius Pintsch.

106 No 6015 *King Richard III*.

107 4½ hours.

108 The Bideford, Westward Ho! and Appledore Railway, closed in 1917.

109 No 2404 *City of Ripon*.

110 Pullman Pups.

111 The elongated 'banjo' dome.

112 1971.

113 The government meat depot in Deptford, south-east London.

114 Georgemas Junction.

115 BR No 62822, originally GNR No 294, built in 1905.

116   The Jungfraujoch terminus of the Jungfrau Railway in Switzerland, at an altitude of 11,333ft, which is actually underground, inside the mountain.

117   Bristol Temple Meads.

118   Cockermouth, where an engine shed was provided for them.

119   *Coronation Scot*, composed by Vivian Ellis.

120   Haydon Square, the site having now been totally obliterated by redevelopment.

121   No 325 had Stephenson valve gear between the frames; No 326 had outside Walschaerts valve gear.

122   Ferrocarril Central de Paraguay, originally the British Paraguay Central Railway.

123   The main line crossed the runways.

124   Paraguay.

125   The Cork & Muskerry Light Railway.

126   Monkton Combe, on the Camerton and Limpley Stoke line.

127   *Royal George*.

128   Stockport.

129   *Hesperus*.

130   Barry Railway, Brecon & Merthyr Railway and Rhymney Railway.

131   'The public be damned'.

132   Lybster, terminus of the Wick & Lybster Light Railway in Caithness.

133   Hawes Junction.

134   The Sligo, Leitrim & Northern Counties Railway.

135   The Henley-on-Thames branch in 1906.

136   John F. McIntosh of the Caledonian Railway.

137   Evercreech Junction.

138   A runaway train at Chapel-en-le-Frith in 1957.

139   They were fitted with streamlining that closely resembled that on the A4 Pacifics.

140   King Frederick IX of Denmark.

RULES

1. The contest is based on correctly answering the prize questions in *The Great Railway Quiz*. Contest and book sales commence 29 April 1984.

2. The book must be purchased to participate in the contest. An original entry form is included in all books. Only original entry forms will be accepted.

3. A ballpoint pen must be used to complete the entry form. The completed entry form should be sent to The Great Railway Quiz, David & Charles Ltd, Brunel House, Forde Road, Newton Abbot, Devon TQ12 1PU.

4. Any entrants under 18 years of age should indicate their age on the entry form and their parent's or guardian's permission to enter.

5. All entries are the property of David & Charles Ltd and none will be returned.

6. No correspondence will be entered into regarding the competition.

7. All entries must be received at the above address no later than 31 December 1984. Any entries arriving after that date will not be accepted. The publishers accept no responsibility for lost or damaged entry forms.

8. Should a tie exist, finalists will be invited to answer additional railway questions supplied by the author. In the event that a tie still exists, a Mastermind-style quiz will take place to decide the winner.

9. Winners will be notified by post.

Entry Form

THE GREAT RAILWAY QUIZ

Print your name and address in the spaces provided and send the completed answer sheet to:

> David & Charles (Great Railway Quiz)
> Brunel House
> Forde Road
> Newton Abbot
> Devon TQ12 1PU

Name ....

Address ....

....

....

....

Telephone (day) .... (evening) ....

Age (if under 18) ....

I hereby give permission for ....

.... to enter *The Great Railway Quiz*.

.... (parent/guardian).

I hereby agree to abide by the rules of the competition.

Signed.........................

Date....................

Closing date for entries 31 December 1984

Diesel and Electric Locomotives and Railways

Q1	A	B	C	D
Q2	A	B	C	D
Q3	A	B	C	D
Q4	A	B	C	D
Q5	A	B	C	D
Q6	A	B	C	D
Q7	A	B	C	D
Q8	A	B	C	D
Q9	A	B	C	D
Q10	A	B	C	D
Q11	A	B	C	D
Q12	A	B	C	D
Q13	A	B	C	D
Q14	A	B	C	D
Q15	A	B	C	D
Q16	A	B	D	D
Q17	A	B	C	D
Q18	A	B	C	D
Q19	A	B	C	D
Q20	A	B	C	D

Miscellany

Q1	A	B	C	D
Q2	A	B	C	D
Q3	A	B	C	D
Q4	A	B	C	D
Q5	A	B	C	D
Q6	A	B	C	D
Q7	A	B	C	D
Q8	A	B	C	D
Q9	A	B	C	D
Q10	A	B	C	D
Q11	A	B	C	D
Q12	A	B	C	D
Q13	A	B	C	D
Q14	A	B	C	D
Q15	A	B	C	D
Q16	A	B	C	D
Q17	A	B	C	D
Q18	A	B	C	D
Q19	A	B	C	D
Q20	A	B	C	D

10. Answers to the prize questions will be printed in the March 1985 issue of *Railway Magazine*.

11. The judges' decision is final.

12. All employees of David & Charles and their families and anyone else connected with the publication *The Great Railway Quiz* are ineligible for the competition.

13. This competition is only open to residents of the United Kingdom and the Republic of Ireland.

ANSWERS

Circle the correct answer with a ballpoint pen

A B Ⓒ D

British Steam Locomotives					**British Railway History**				
Q1	A	B	C	D	**Q1**	A	B	C	D
Q2	A	B	C	D	**Q2**	A	B	C	D
Q3	A	B	C	D	**Q3**	A	B	C	D
Q4	A	B	C	D	**Q4**	A	B	C	D
Q5	A	B	C	D	**Q5**	A	B	C	D
Q6	A	B	C	D	**Q6**	A	B	C	D
Q7	A	B	C	D	**Q7**	A	B	C	D
Q8	A	B	C	D	**Q8**	A	B	C	D
Q9	A	B	C	D	**Q9**	A	B	C	D
Q10	A	B	C	D	**Q10**	A	B	C	D
Q11	A	B	C	D	**Q11**	A	B	C	D
Q12	A	B	C	D	**Q12**	A	B	C	D
Q13	A	B	C	D	**Q13**	A	B	C	D
Q14	A	B	C	D	**Q14**	A	B	C	D
Q15	A	B	C	D	**Q15**	A	B	C	D
Q16	A	B	D	D	**Q16**	A	B	C	D
Q17	A	B	C	D	**Q17**	A	B	C	D
Q18	A	B	C	D	**Q18**	A	B	C	D
Q19	A	B	C	D	**Q19**	A	B	C	D
Q20	A	B	C	D	**Q20**	A	B	C	D

British Railway Engineering				**Foreign Railways**			
Q1 A B C D				**Q1** A B C D			
Q2 A B C D				**Q2** A B C D			
Q3 A B C D				**Q3** A B C D			
Q4 A B C D				**Q4** A B C D			
Q5 A B C D				**Q5** A B C D			
Q6 A B C D				**Q6** A B C D			
Q7 A B C D				**Q7** A B C D			
Q8 A B C D				**Q8** A B C D			
Q9 A B C D				**Q9** A B C D			
Q10 A B C D				**Q10** A B C D			
Q11 A B C D				**Q11** A B C D			
Q12 A B C D				**Q12** A B C D			
Q13 A B C D				**Q13** A B C D			
Q14 A B C D				**Q14** A B C D			
Q15 A B C D				**Q15** A B C D			
Q16 A B D D				**Q16** A B C D			
Q17 A B C D				**Q17** A B C D			
Q18 A B C D				**Q18** A B C D			
Q19 A B C D				**Q19** A B C D			
Q20 A B C D				**Q20** A B C D			